BEING
Your Self

BEING
Your Self

Seeing and Knowing
What's IN the Way
IS the Way

Liberation from **EGO**

Healing Your **EMOTIONS**

Renewing Your **ENERGY**

MIKE GEORGE

BEING Your Self

Seeing and Knowing

What's IN the Way
IS the Way!

Liberation from EGO - Healing Your EMOTIONS

Renewing Your ENERGY

Mike George

Text Copyright Mike George 2014

Print Edition ISBN: 978-0-9576673-3-4

Also available as an E-Book

First published by Gavisus Media 2014
Level 14, Boulevard Plaza One
Emmar Boulevard
Downtown Dubai
PO Box 691400 Dubai, UAE

Email: gavisusmedia@gmail.com

The moral rights of the author have been asserted.

Cover Design: Charlotte Mouncey - www.bookstyle.co.uk

The information given in this book should not be treated as a substitute for professional medical advice; always consult a medical practitioner. Any use of information in this book is at the reader's discretion and risk. Neither the author nor the publisher can be held responsible for any loss, claim or damage arising out of use, or misuse, or the suggestions made or the failure to take medical advice

Other Books by Mike George

The Immune System of the SOUL
How to Free Your Self from ALL Forms of Dis - ease

The 7 Myths About LOVE...Actually!
The Journey from Your HEAD to the HEART of Your SOUL

Don't Get MAD Get Wise
Why no one ever makes you angry...ever!

The 7 AHA!s of Highly Enlightened Souls
How to Free YOUR Self from ALL Forms of Stress

Learn to Find Inner Peace
Manage your anxieties, think well, feel well.

Learn to Relax
Ease tension, conquer stress and free the self

In the Light of Meditation
A guide to meditation and spiritual development

1001 Ways to Relax
Beat stress and find perfect calm, anywhere, anytime

1001 Meditations
Discover peace of mind

Subscribe to Clear Thinking

Clear Thinking is a regular e-article (once or twice a month) that
Mike currently circulates to around 15,000 people worldwide. Topics
vary, but they all serve to sustain the ongoing learning and unlearning
that is required to restore your capacity to be your self.

If you would like to subscribe, go to www.relax7.com or send an email
to **mike@relax7.com** - it's free.

Contents

Part FOUR

Emotional CONTAGION

Part FIVE

Renewing Your ENERGY

Part SIX

BIG QUESTIONS

Part SEVEN

The Epilogue and The Essence

Waking up!

In the physical dimension, in the universe of your bed,
while you sleep you dream.

In your dream you believe you are awake.

Only to be awakened from your dream
to discover you were really asleep.

In the spiritual dimension, which is the universe of your
consciousness, (which is you) while you believe you are awake
it's really a dream.

You dream the world because you filter it through your perception,
which is largely shaped by your ego,
which is an 'unreal' version of you!

This ensures you will create an 'unreal' version of
everything and everyone else.

What you believe is real is unreal, but you don't know it.

Your consequent suffering makes your waking dream
often seem like a nightmare.

The nightmare is tolerable, until it's not.

This ensures that one day you will start to
question the nature of reality.

As you do you will begin to awaken from the dream
that you thought was real.

How fast can you awaken is not the right question!

How do you know when you are awake?

This is the question!

Can You KNOW the Truth About YOU?

Why do we sometimes react to another person just on seeing them? Why do we become emotional at the sight of another's sorrow? Why do we surrender to the movie and then make ourselves frightened or tearful while we know it's just a movie? Why do we need to pay someone else to find out what happened in our past that is ruling our present? Why don't all those methods and techniques of self-change, carrying the promise of your 'power unleashed' and 'potential fulfilled', not achieve the transformation in our feelings and our life that they promise and that we seek?

There are probably a hundred other similar questions being asked every day by thousands of people on-line, off-line, down the line and along that line we call the bottom line! They arise as the result of our search to fill the big hole that we all seem to be left with when we suddenly realize we are all grown up! It's that great big vacant space in the middle of almost all our lives called 'self-understanding'. Just over thirty years ago I noticed the presence of that hole. I realized the cause of my high levels of stress were due to my ignorance of me! So 'feeling' the call to find out why my life was joyless and making no sense, I set off around the world to find 'the truth'! I would eventually realize it was a naïve decision as I discovered the truth that I sought was not 'out there' somewhere in the universe. It is embedded in the heart of each and every one of us. It belongs to no religion, no philosophy and certainly no individual, regardless of how greatly they may be esteemed by others. Truth is not a theory, philosophy or concept.

In this, as in all my other attempts at writing, I do not intend to tell you the truth. As more seekers are beginning to realize, the truth cannot be told. It cannot be captured in words. Only pointed at. I only share with you my own discoveries and realizations, some insights and perhaps a little accumulated wisdom.

Experience tells me one of the ways we can each rediscover and realize what is *true* is to uncover and identify our inherited and learned *beliefs*. Then, to 'see beyond and behind' those beliefs through practices such as meditation, contemplation and deep conversations with others. It's easy to become a consumer of others realizations and reflections, believing them to be empowering. It's easy to gorge on the wisdom of others and suffer from a form of intellectual indigestion. Creating a balanced diet of the wisdom of others, alongside your own personal reflections, integrated into your daily practices of meditation and contemplation, seems to generate the necessary realizations of what is true for you.

Why should you seek your own deeper truths? You probably recognize that the mental and intellectual forces in the world are now more than slightly haywire, on a grand scale! We have more information but seem to be less wise; we are more comfortable but seem to be less happy; there is incredible progress in technology but there seems to be more disconnection and conflict in our relationships; the environment is telling us to stop plundering and our hearts are telling us to calm down – but we seem to be incapable of doing either. Most of us are addicted to our emotions and the ego is running riot in almost every area of society. But that's 'out there' and it's all just a distraction until we fully understand what, in truth, is going on 'in here', in our own hearts and minds.

This book as not designed to be a definitive text that delivers answers or magical techniques. It contains only insights, observations and realizations from my own reflective and meditative practice while engaging with the wisdom of the wise!

Please do not 'believe' a word that you read. We have enough beliefs. See for your self! When you do then your thoughts, feelings and actions follow. In fact it's 'belief' that is slowly strangling our energy and it's belief that we use to justify strangling others. Better to use the words here as assists or signposts. Before being your self comes seeing for your self! But first, let's fully define the challenge embedded in the title. It's a challenge that we all seem to be facing whether we are aware of it or not!

BEING YOUR SELF

It's not easy to be your self. Most days it seems like everyone wants you to be someone else as they project their version of you on to you!

We are surrounded and ambushed every day by a thousand images and voices all calling us to invest our identity in their product, their brand, their label, their service. They know that if we do they will gain access to our pockets. They are not easy to resist!

Almost every movie has been carefully crafted to suck you in and have you live through one or perhaps many characters, as if you are them! You are invited to 'go through' their adventures and their traumas, to identify with their emotional aches and pains and feel what they feel. It is an illusion of an illusion that is both addictive and exhausting. It's not easy to look away!

Most of the modern music that captures our attention hooks us with a combination of lyric and sound that we find easy to resonate with. We wrap our self in the music and live through the words, for a few moments at least. We make 'this track' the soundtrack of our life... for a few moments at least! It's not easy to turn it off! It's not easy not to want to listen again, and again! Even those shinny magazine people have trained us to admire and aspire to be and live like the glossy people on their glossy pages. We project our sense of self into their apparently glossy lifestyle with both a sense of wonder and a desire to be like 'them'. It's not easy, for many, to deny themselves their 'glossy fix'.

And there we all were, prior to our entry into the big wide adult world, with all it's attempts to shape our sense of self, at the mercy our parents and teachers who spent so much time asking us and telling us what we could be, should be, would be! It wasn't easy to notice, especially in such formative years, their projection of their aspirations into our life. More than likely it just fogged our ability to be our self and see for our self. It wasn't easy to ignore them!

So it's not surprising we will all go through our own unique form of identity crisis. Some of us, at some point, will even find ourselves screaming out to the world in our own brand of frustration, "Who the hell am I?" Others just keep it all inside and develop a coping strategy while suppressing the frustrations. Some will become so inwardly confused and disorientated, perhaps inventing multiple selves, they may start to speak and behave in ways that society will call deviant. It is from their condition that the psychiatrists and therapists will earn their daily crust. And then there are the vast majority of 'us' who will live our entire life not realizing that all our angers and fears, all our reactions and rages, all our discontentments and avoidances, all our unhappy encounters, in short, all our stress and suffering, is all down to one thing. We don't know who we really are! But it's not easy to make that connection!

There is even likely to be one of those moments when, in preparing anxiously for an interview or nervously for a presentation, a friend will say, "Relax, you'll be fine, just be your self". Our immediate thought will sound like, "Yes of course, I just need to relax and be my self". But it doesn't take long before the mental tsunami arrives screaming, "Yes but what does that mean? What does it mean to be my self? How do I be myself? I don't know how to be me!

Wait a minute, who am I". Not only does the anxiety flood back in but the deepest existential enquiry is now underway in our own heads! But it's not easy to maintain the 'who am I' enquiry as by now we have learned and developed many efficient habits of losing our self in something or someone that we are not! Otherwise known as 'escape'!

Have you ever wondered why you 'seem' to be a different person in the presence of different people? Have you ever noticed how often you look for others to affirm who you are? Have you ever asked your self, "Has who I thought I was changed"? If so who did you think you were, and who do you think you are now? Have you ever listed all the things upon which you base and build your sense of identity?

And so it is, that we can easily live our entire life and never be who we truly are. Looking for your self doesn't help!

SEEING YOUR SELF

You can never see your own face. Except perhaps for the very end of your nose! You can only ever see a 'reflection' of your face. Can the eye see the eye? Obviously not, as it is the eye that is looking? Similarly, you can never 'see' your self. The self is not your face! The self is the being, the 'I' that says 'I am'! The I cannot see the I, for it is the I that is looking... for the I!

The only way you can see your self is in the reflection that comes back from the mirrors that are your relationships. But like the physical equivalent it will be a superficial representation, distorted by the curvature of the mirrors. Others vision of you will be distorted by the complexity and confusion already existent within 'them'! They will see you in a way that is colored by what they believe themselves to be. In other words if they don't know themselves accurately they will reflect an inaccurate sense of you. That's why looking in the mirror of others to get a sense of your self, will always give you in inaccurate and distorted view. Phew!

Almost no one has a truly clear view of anything or anyone because they not able to consistently be themselves. Our perception and therefore our vision of others is always clouded by our own sense of self, which is, as we will see, not real, not true. This is not easy to 'see' as it is so close to home! But while it's a personal affliction it's also a flaw that is operating within human consciousness on a global scale! Hence the somewhat chaotic state of human affairs in the world today!

'Seeing' is something we tend to associate only with our physical eyes. But as the being of consciousness that we are, in order to 'see', in order to gain insight, we use our third eye, often called the eye of the intellect. Seeing is perceiving, it is touching and feeling what is happening within our consciousness, that is, within our self. All you can ever see is what you create within your consciousness, within your 'self'. And the creator is not the creation. Your creation, as in your thoughts and feelings, perceptions and emotions, can only ever be a representation of you, the creator, according to your current belief about your self, about who and what you are. And as long as you carry any 'belief about' your self then you can never truly be your self. You will always be trying to 'be the belief'. And the self is not a belief! This is why self-belief has its limitations and will ultimately get in the way of you being your authentic self!

If there is such a thing as the 'spiritual journey' then seeing the many beliefs and subtle illusions that we have learned to create about our self is the result of spiritual practice while walking a spiritual path.

It's those illusions about who and what you are that are 'in the way' of you being able to be your self. It's an illusion to consider your self to be anything other that what 'you are', which is simply awareness itself. We may say that, "I am a spiritual being, or that I am a soul or that I am simply the 'I' that says 'I am'". None of these descriptions are wrong and they are certainly more accurate than believing that you are what you see in the bathroom mirror. But even these ideas and 'concepts' of being spirit, being soul, being the 'I' that says I am, have to go if we are to be...me! For they are ideas and concepts, trapped in words, and the self is not an idea or a concept.

The paradox of this 'inner seeing' is that all you can ever see (perceive) is what is not you! All you can see is what is occurring within you. Then, in the process of seeing you may notice that you are the seer. That's all! Yet, therein lies a natural serenity, a lightness of being, the 'ultimate freedom'. Therein lies what makes the walking of the spiritual path worthwhile.

KNOWING YOUR SELF

When it is fully realized that you cannot see your 'self' the implications are, well, enormous. The first is that you can never know your self. How can the knower know how to make the knower something that is known? It's impossible. An aspect of that 'ultimate freedom' is realizing that you don't need to.

When you talk 'about your self' notice you are usually talking about what you feel or think, what you remember or desire, or who you 'believe' you are. They are your creation, but they are not you, the authentic self. You can see and know the quality of your creation but you cannot see or know your self. The creator is not the creation.

As the 'knower' you can only know what is not you. But it takes a little practice to recognize that. It takes practice to not be fooled into believing one knows one's self. That practice allows you to see and know that your habits of belief, perception, thought and action are not 'you'. They all change, but you don't!

Only when all that is mistaken for self is seen and known for what it is i.e. illusion, can the self be the self! That's also the moment when all desires and urges to see and know anything, are emptied out of our consciousness. The self is naked and is 'felt' to be nothing more than pure awareness. Seeing and knowing what is not you allows you to fully realize what's IN the way IS the way of that nakedness! This realization can occur through a practiced process of elimination e.g. this image is not me, this feeling is not me, etc. It can occur as an instant glimpse and the recognition that any belief about your self is not true! Either way it seems some form of meditation is necessary to facilitate this personal seeing and knowing of what is not me!

Some say meditation is the cultivation of self-awareness. That's OK. For beginners! But eventually the self realizes the self IS awareness itself, and all that the self can be aware of is what is 'in' awareness. And what is 'in awareness' is never the self! Clear? Of course not! If it were you would probably be sitting on your mountain peak radiating your enlightenment outwards and across the world. You certainly would not be reading books!

So what is the purpose of this book? It's a set of linguistic signposts that point and recommend you look with your inner eye at this, at that, then there and then here, within your consciousness, within your self. As you do you will start to see for your self and know for your self what you are putting in the way of being your self. Then, you may realize that you can only get OUT of the way what IS in the way by your seeing and knowing that what 'appears' to be IN the way, 'in reality'... isn't!

Do let me know what you see, if you feel inclined. Do let me know if the signs you find within this book are blurred, or seem to be taking you in a direction away from seeing and knowing what's IN the way! What's IN the way is always the same. It just takes many forms. It is always our oldest a dearest companion. The ego.

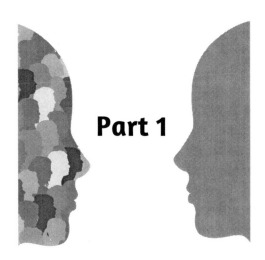

Part 1

The Ego's Games

It's what's IN the Way!

Seven insights into how we LOSE our Way

Insight ONE

The Cause of Our Illusions, Delusions and Confusions

The ego is neither good nor bad, positive nor negative. It is simply a case of mistaken identity. We have all seen the hypnotist convincing a group of people who, at the snap of his fingers, will all stand up and act like King Henry or Queen Mary, or delight in eating a raw onion believing it to be an apple! The ego is the ultimate in self-hypnosis. We learn to convince our self we are someone that we are not, without being aware that we do so! We will ultimately and unknowingly create many 'selves', then wonder why it's so hard to be natural, to 'be authentic', to be me. This is the nature of the journey 'into' self-confusion and then 'out to' a world full of confused people. It seems to be a journey that we all make to some extent or other.

I too was one of those confused people. I still occasionally relapse into allowing an illusory self (often various selves) to cloud my mind, distort my intellect and infect my heart. But it's progressively less frequent and thankfully each 'episode' lasts a shorter time. It seems most of us just don't realize we are suffering from a severe case of 'multiple mistaken identities'! As we create those many selves, many versions of 'me', most of us seem unable to make the connection between 'many me's' and all our many moments, perhaps a lifetime of moments, of unhappiness.

Such is the subtle power of the ego that apparently intelligent people don't realize they are confused. Those few that do mostly don't know why the ego is the cause or how to awaken from their confusion. Fortunately this loss of true self-awareness is always temporary, simply because it is illusory. It's just that 'temporary' can still mean a long stretch of corporeal time, and for some, the entire time of their life! It's always the creation of an 'illusory self' that sabotages the energy of our true nature and, as we shall see, distorts it into many forms of emotional pain.

In this first section we explore, reveal, dissolve and hopefully 'taste' the end of the ego as we go in search of the greatest prize at this time. It's not love. It's not peace. It's not even happiness. It is liberation from self-created suffering. Everything else follows. Understand the ego and you understand almost everything. No one is truly a free being as long as they still create a false sense of self within their consciousness. But it's a habit that is hard to kick. It's also a habit that ensures authentic happiness remains as rare as a four-leafed clover!

Only a soul liberated from ego can know peace, live with love, and be happy, for no particular reason!

Our Long-term Companion

Some say it is impossible to be free of ego. They contend that it's a necessary part of day-to-day life. They say that we need an ego to get through our average day, which requires we dance across many identities. They say that the ego will therefore be with us till the end of our days, so we might as well just get used to it. But that may just be a neat way of justifying not making the effort to wake up and stay awake - rather like finding the perfect excuse to stay in bed in the morning! It is more likely a subconscious way to avoid being a fully free being and then fulfilling the responsibilities that come with that level of freedom. It may also be a way to 'hang on' to our suffering, to our stress, to our unhappiness, which have become habitual and paradoxically woven into our comfort zones!

Most of us have had moments when our spirit soared, when we felt and knew the highest spiritual freedom; moments when we were free of all fear; moments when we were enthusiastically curious; moments when both sadness and anger were impossible; moments when we gave of our self, free of wanting anything in return. These are egoless moments. These are moments when we were our authentic self again. Can we move our self into such moments? Can we create such moments? Can we expand such moments? There is only one answer!

Our Favorite Miscreation

Whenever you identify with something that you are not then you 'create ego'. The pathway to freedom begins with being aware enough to notice how and why you lose your 'sense of self', your identity, in what you are not, hundreds of times every day!

It is this *illusory* sense of self that then generates certain emotional 'disturbances' such as fear, sadness and anger, which many of us have also learned to believe are not only normal but necessary, and even desired. This is *delusional* thinking for it is such emotions that blind us and prevent us from thinking and acting in alignment with the 'truth', the truth being our true state of being. In this true state we have no identity!

Yes, ultimately you and I have no identity. The being of consciousness that you and I are, has no identity. To realize that, to live from that state, is to be your self. However, just the 'idea' of being without an identity, of being identitiless, does not compute easily within our rational minds. After a lifetime of 'multiple identity creation', in a world where governments, organisations, businessess and our livelihoods all depend on each one of us 'assuming' many different identities, we learn to believe that we have to 'be somebody'. This one belief ensures we will remain fast asleep to who we really are.

We are each an individual and unique conscious being. We can use different words to describe the being of consciousness that we are. Words like soul, spirit or psyche do the job. Some prefer the 'authentic self'. Others refer to the 'I' that says 'I Am'. The soul/self/spirit, (which is you) in your original and true state of being, has no identity. Identities are only created and maintained when the soul/self comes into and animates the form that we call 'my body'. It is the body to which we assign an identity and eventually many other identities will follow based on the characteristics or 'extensions' of the form we occupy.

Radiant Beings
The true nature of every conscious being is to openly 'radiate' the energy of consciousness, the energy of the self. We radiate outwards. We are here to give the energy of our self. When we do, in our own natural way, we feel connected and at one with others, while maintaining a separate sense of self. When we do that freely we are content and at peace within our self, simply because it's our nature. Those who receive our radiant, untainted energy, experience what we refer to as love. But the ego, that illusory sense of self that we create within our consciousness, reverses all that. It distorts the energy of our consciousness, and we generate and radiate the intention of desire and the emotions of fear and anger instead. We become discontent because we want something from others that will affirm our illusory sense of self. We desire some feedback or some signs that will strengthen a fabricated definition of 'me'. And when we don't get it we start to radiate anxiety and resentment.

Chaos in society becomes inevitable when this personal loss of true self-awareness occurs across the 'collective'. All conflict arises between human beings because they are identifying their 'self' with something they are not! Yet this is what we are all taught to do. All forms and levels of violence in the world have only this one root cause - the ego! Hence the need for rules and laws in every society, in order to maintain some kind of order and harmony between humans who have forgotten how to be... human!

That's why realizing and remembering who 'I am', in reality, is recognized as the spiritual way to restore peace to a peaceless world. Peace treaties don't work. Trying to fix others doesn't work. Playing politics doesn't work. Going to war for peace has never worked. It's only when the self is liberated from ego that it's possible to understand, accept and embrace ALL others, regardless of how big or deep or many-faced the egos of those 'others' are.

Joining the Dots

In the following pages we will join the dots between Ego and Emotion to see how one arises out of the other. We will see exactly how and why we create our own emotional suffering. We will pinpoint the natural spiritual laws of consciousness that are permanently 'built into' our being. If our thoughts, feelings and behaviors are not aligned with these innate laws, we will misuse and waste our energy and personal suffering, disharmony between people and the disintegration of society are guaranteed.

First up, it's our old friend the EGO. What exactly is the EGO and how exactly do we create it? Why do we lose our ability to 'be in' our true state of consciousness? Why do we create a false identity in a hundred ways, hundreds of times every day, and not even realize that we do so? Unless we see and understand this process of 'miscreation' we will not be able to free our self from our inner prison. There will always be something IN the way. Consequently, we may never know true love or authentic happiness in our own life.

As we enter the territory of consciousness, the 'inner space' with which we are mostly unfamiliar, I would recommend you STOP reading frequently. Take many moments to look within and pay attention to what is in your awareness, in you. Then you may see the reality of what I am describing for your self, within your self, within you, the powerful being of consciousness that you are.

At the end of many of the short chapters there is an invitation to undertake a short exercise to assist you in your contemplations and to create your own realizations. Here is the first.

PAUSE

Take a moment to write down your definition of the EGO. There is no right answer. I have yet to meet two people who have 'exactly' the same definition or description. See if you can sense what the ego is and how you create it.

Insight TWO

What are YOU... really?

The oldest riddle! What is known by many, but realized by few? Answer: What you are! Most people know in their heart of hearts that they are not what they see reflecting back to them in the shop window as they walk by! It's simply a transient material form that is born, ages and dies. Deep down we all know, but have yet to fully realize and remember, that we are the energy that animates the form that we see. When this is fully realized it changes almost everything!

You are the occupier of a country called 'material form'. The 'energy of you', however, is called by many other names. Consciousness, soul, spirit, heart (not the heart of your body!), authentic self are the most common.

As the 'self' is entirely non-physical you cannot 'scientifically' prove your existence as a being of consciousness and 'no thing' else. But you can prove it to your self by becoming 'aware' that you are the being within the form. Self-awareness allows you to know that you are not just a form that contains some mysterious being! You are the dweller, the driver, the animator, of form. Scientists sometimes refer to this invisible entity as the 'ghost in the machine'. They see the body as a wondrous machine to be measured, calibrated and understood in all its complexity, in the minutest of detail. But they cannot fathom what brings it to life! So they refer to a 'ghost' in the machine, a mysterious, unseen and yet vital energy that enlivens the form and keeps the body... alive! That's you!

In most spiritual traditions, that 'ghost' is simply understood to be the soul or spirit – invisible, intangible and internally situated in the brain. But it's not the brain itself! Realization of this is helped by the practice of regular meditation and contemplation. These practices expand self-awareness and bring you to self-realization. That's the AHA! moment when you realize that you are an energy that is much bigger, much greater, much more subtle, much more powerful, than the small, physical superficial energetic object called a body! Sometimes this realization is called 'soul consciousness'.

Knowing Your Self as You Are!

You CAN know that the energy of you is quite different from the energy of the form that you occupy. You CAN know that you are of another dimension. Your body has to be in the room where it is right now. It cannot be anywhere else. But YOU can leave the room in one second. Sometimes, when you drift off, when you become absent, someone notices and says, "Are you still with me?" In a split second you return to the room and to the person speaking to you. In that moment you become aware you went somewhere. You know not where or for how long you were away! You went into another dimension beyond the awareness of time and space. Matter cannot do that, a physical body cannot do that, which indicates that YOU are not a material entity confined to space and time!

In a state of 'soul consciousness' you remain aware that you don't have a soul you ARE the soul, that you are not your body but the animator of the body! It's just that when you are in that awareness you are not thinking it! And you can't 'think' your way into it! It's an elusive state of consciousness, not least because we have spent our entire life under the illusion that we are just a set of measurements based on the height, width and the physical features that we see in the bathroom mirror every day! It's just a habit to perceive your self in that way.

Up to now we have been living from a state of 'body consciousness'. That's the state in which you believe you are just your body. It's a 'belief', with virus-like attributes, that has spread to infect the consciousness of almost every human being.

When we all share this one single illusion it results in two global phenomena. We become totally obsessed by all things material. 'Possession and ownership' become the imperatives of daily life, which drive us to collectively co-create a world of continuous consumption and accumulation. This creates almost continuous conflict, extreme suffering and tremendous inequality. It is a viral belief that makes us live by material values alone. Even when we espouse the beauty and greatness of spirit in our writings and conversations, we will likely still 'act' as if the physical is primary, as if we are just a material form. 'I am just this body' is therefore a belief that kills our ability to interact in ways that we call truthful, moral and ethical. It ensures we will think, speak and act mostly in self-serving ways, with selfish intentions, in order to survive and thrive at a physical level.

I am this body is a belief that spawns many other beliefs including: it's survival of the fittest; you have to look after number one; survive or die; you have to be physically beautiful to be happy and successful. Little do we realize that believing we are only a material form will guarantee a life of stress, emotional suffering and many shocking surprises that ensure unhappiness will be our companion along the way.

PAUSE

Take a moment to reflect on your average day. What do you think about the most? Write a list and put next to each item a rough percentage of your daily attention that you give to each area/item. Then tick the ones that are 'material'. Then work out the rough percentage of your day that goes on materially focused or related thinking.

What actually happens within YOU?

Have you ever noticed what is 'happening' within your consciousness, within YOU? There are always events in the world that seem to be 'out there'. But there are also 'events' in the world within your consciousness 'in here'. Take a moment to be aware of what is happening within you and you will notice that ALL events, even the ones that you believe are happening 'out there' are, in reality, happening within YOU! You will notice that as you perceive the world you create the world. As you perceive people and events, objects and circumstances, you are creating them within the inner world of your consciousness.

There is a need to 'see' and understand this perceptive/creative process if you are to stop allowing your self to be hypnotized into a state based on an illusory version of... you! For example if someone says you are Spanish you 'create' a self-image/belief/concept of your self as a Spanish person. But that's not true. It's an illusion. Nationality is just an idea. It's an illusory idea that you create within your consciousness about your self. It's a false identity!

Let's say the person sitting next to you watching television is under the illusion that they are Canadian. When you watch the news on television your reactions to some events will be different from that person. If a hurricane has destroyed the coastline of Spain and you see your self as Spanish then you will likely create a highly emotional reaction to the event. Whereas the person whose sense of identity is based on 'I am Canadian' will not create the event, or their response, in the same way! They are perceiving/creating the events and therefore their interpretation of events differently from you. Both of you are carrying a different sense of self, which is the primary filter through which you bring the world and thereby create what's happening in the world... in you!

When you sit quietly and just watch what is happening within your consciousness you will start to see what you do *with* your mind, *in* your mind and *on* your mind! You will notice that you are not your mind. You will notice that you create your mind and then use your mind to create your version of the world and therefore your thoughts about the world, according to how you see your self, according to who or what you 'believe' you are. Here's a good metaphor to understand how the mind works, and then how you use your mind, within your consciousness, within YOU.

The Mind at Work

It's only quite recently that cars have been developed which, when standing at the traffic lights, automatically switch off their own engines to save fuel. Then, as soon as you put the foot on the accelerator, the engine starts up automatically. No need to turn any key on or off. It's as if the engine received a subliminal message when it's time to start moving, then it starts itself automatically. Similarly, when you think, when you create a thought, a wave of energy arises from within your consciousness. It's a wave within the energy of you, sometimes we call it a vibration, that becomes a thought. In that instant your mind comes into existence in order to receive this arising 'thought wave' and to give the thought a form. Not a physical form but a form in the energy of consciousness, the energy of you. These 'thought forms' can be ideas, images, concepts etc. If you stopped thinking you would have no mind. You wouldn't need one as there would be no thoughts to be given form!

Just as the car engine switches itself off when it's not needed, so the mind disappears when it's not needed. But you, the being of consciousness, always remains! This is one reason why your mind is not a function of your brain, it's a faculty of your consciousness, of you!

So essentially the mind is a faculty that arises within consciousness, within you, in order to 'think'. Having said that, here's the interesting bit. When you are 'thinking' it's as if YOU can be fully aware that there are thoughts arising within you. It's as if there is you and then there are your thoughts. It's as if you are able to watch your own creation: i.e. thoughts arising, taking form, appearing and passing across an inner screen called the mind. It could be likened to sitting in a cinema, or in front of the TV, watching images pass across the screen. The mind is your canvas and your thoughts are your painting. It's just that in the cinema the screen, the chair, your body and your eyes are all separate. But in your consciousness, you, your mind and your thoughts are all ONE!

The Interface between You and the World!

Your mind is also the interface between you 'in here' so to speak, and the world 'out there'. You receive the world 'out there' on the screen of your mind 'in here'. Notice the next time you daydream. While you may be looking out into the world through the physical eyes of your body, there is something else on your mind. Perhaps an old series of images have been dragged up from the archives, called memory, and are being reviewed. Perhaps a worry is taking the form of some dark mental images. So while your eyes are looking out and receiving the 'incoming world', you are busy creating and watching entirely unrelated thoughts and images on your mind. Sometimes others notice, and ask you, "You seem to have something on your mind, do you want to talk about it?" That's when you notice you just drifted off into some random thoughts and suddenly you refocus your attention to the world 'out there'. In an instant you become fully aware of the incoming images and sounds of the external world. Then you start to create thoughts 'in here', in your mind, 'about' the world out there. That's when you may realize the world out there is really 'in here'!

You are not an Image

So when someone asks you, "Who are you, really?", here is what usually happens. You translate their 'who are you?' question into a thought 'who am I?'. That triggers a memory in your subconscious, which throws up a previously created thought/s and the previously recorded answer. You then describe your self according to what you have thought/said before. This is usually based on what you were told and taught in the past, which is an idea about your self, which you now hold as your 'belief' about who you are. And you say, "I am... followed by a label or a concept about you"! But, in truth, whatever you put after the 'I AM' is not you. It's just an idea, a concept, a belief, a label, perhaps an image. And YOU are not an idea, you are not a concept, label, belief or an image. You are... you! You 'create' ideas and images, you generate beliefs, you record and remember them, and then recreate them. But you are the creator, and the creator is not the creation! And yet the creation is 'happening' within the creator!

PAUSE

Take a moment, and see if you can see the dynamic described above within your self, within your consciousness. Sit quietly and watch your self receive the world out there 'in here', and then how you create your version of it within you, on the screen of your mind. Notice the beliefs and biases that are already recorded within you that are shaping your creation of the world out there... in here, right now!

Mind How You Be!

One of the great confusions, even in so-called spiritual circles, is that you are your mind. 'Believing' that 'mind' is just an aspect of brain function makes it even harder to see for your self that you 'emerge a faculty called mind' within your consciousness, within you, in order to think. The mind is essentially your thinking ability/capacity. But it's not you! Well it is, but it's not!

Why do we need to think? Because we don't 'understand' and we believe we need to think our way to understanding! We cannot perceive clearly and we do not know with clarity! We believe that we need to know, so we search for what we believe we need to know using thought. For example: you know what a bed sheet is, you know why it should be washed and you know how to wash it. So you do not create thoughts about it or how it becomes clean. You just do it. You clean it. But do you know who you are and why you are here? Do you understand how life works and how to live with others? Mostly we don't know, and therefore we do not understand who we are or how life works. So instead of sitting quietly in order to 'see and realize' who we are and how life works, we just 'think' about it.

We try to 'think' our way to seeing and knowing and understanding. But you cannot know or understand anything by thinking. But we don't know that so we become frustrated, perplexed, lost. So we think some more! We go round in circles and become tired and stressed. Then we meekly surrender to other people's thoughts, other people's descriptions, perceptions and conclusions. We absorb other people's beliefs, re-create them and claim them as our own, and then convince our self that we know! But we don't. We just believe we know. When you really do 'know' you don't need to believe and thinking becomes irrelevant, redundant. How do you know? You don't, until you 'see' and realize this for your self!

Insight **FOUR**

What is the EGO exactly
and how do we create it... precisely?

Ego has a number of definitions and descriptions. It is a false sense of self. It is a sense of identity, which is not true. It is an identity created by and within the spiritual energy sometimes referred to as the self/soul/spirit when we identify with something that we are not. Ego is, to borrow a phrase from New Scotland Yard, simply a 'case of mistaken identity'. Or, in one single word, it is simply a 'mistake'! Here is a slightly longer description. It also contains the mechanism by which we create an ego.

EGO is the attachment to and identification
with an image/idea/concept/belief in your mind.

We learn to believe that we are an 'idea' about our self that we create in our mind. But we don't realize it's just an idea and that the idea is not me! We identify our self with our own thoughts, our own creation. Sometimes I use the term 'wrong image' above, for those just beginning to be interested in the inner territory of consciousness! Many therefore ask me (but not usually the beginners), "Well what is the 'right' image/idea to be attached to and identified with"? The answer is, no image or idea! The self is not an image. You have no image. But that's not so easy to see! Our whole life is a hypnotic conditioning in which we learn to associate and identify our self with an image or an idea or a concept that we ourselves create in our mind. Most of us will learn to be highly 'image conscious'.

We then project that image, often expressed in the form of a belief about our self, out into the world, in order to make an impression on others in the world. Sometimes we call it self-belief! But we don't normally realize, until it's too late, that this is the pathway to much stress and tension, struggle and unhappiness. Why, because a) the self is not a belief and b) if there is self-belief there must be self-doubt. So we then seek and become dependent upon others affirmation and approval of our self-belief/self-image to avoid the suffering of self-doubt!

Back to the Movie

Let's return to the cinema metaphor for a moment. You are sitting watching the movie. At the start of the movie you are fully aware that you are in your seat watching the movie. You are aware that up there, on the screen, a story is unfolding in colored flickering light. But you are not so aware that the story is actually appearing on the screen of your mind. That's what you are looking at with your inner eye.

After a few moments you lose the awareness of your self, your body, the seat, the auditorium and the screen. Suddenly it's as if 'you' are up there in the movie. But in reality 'you' have just gone into the images, into the story, in your own 'mind'. When the hero cries you cry, when the hero is scared you get scared, when the hero is angry you become upset too. In reality the movie isn't out there. You bring it into you and you 'play' your version of the movie ON the screen of your mind. Then YOU go into the movie, into the story, that's playing IN your mind. You lose your SELF in the story that you are now creating in your mind. Suddenly you are adopting the identity of the hero character for a few moments, then the identity of the hero's lover for a few moments, then the bad guy for a few moments, etc.

How do you know you are losing your 'self' in what's 'on' your mind? You become emotional! You generate emotions as a result of your identification with some of the character's words and actions in the movie. You create emotion when something happens to the character that you most identify with. You feel those emotions, usually as sadness or fear, perhaps frustration or anger. You believe you are being moved by the movie. You may even say, "I was so moved"! But the movie didn't move you, you moved you! You moved your self into your version of the story in your mind, then into the character, then identified your 'self' with the character. Then, when something happened to the character, you created your own version of what happened (in your mind) as if it was happening to you, and then you... emoted!

Now in Slow Motion

Lets see how that works in the day-to-day world of work and home. Someone comes to visit. They spill coffee all over your new white pristine and perfect carpet. You become angry. "You should be more careful", you shout in your anger! In that moment are you in a state of pleasure or pain? Pain of course. More accurately, you are suffering. Who caused your suffering? Not the visitor, and not the coffee. Not even gravity! You did. Why? Because, for a few moments, you were a carpet! That's why you took it so personally.

So let's slow that down as we explore the mechanics of the process. You are you, the being of consciousness. You have a mind within your being. In your mind you create the thought, the idea, the image, of a nice new white carpet. Whenever you look at the carpet you bring the carpet into your mind and then YOU go into your mind and then YOU go into the image of the carpet on your mind. This is called 'attachment'. This is where attachment happens. Whatever 'you' become attached to in your mind, you will also identify with. But that's quite subtle and it happens so fast you are not aware that that is what YOU are doing within the energy of consciousness that you are. You don't consciously think 'I am a carpet' but the habit of losing your self in an image on your mind is almost the same. You lose your sense of self in what's 'on' your mind. Just like you get lost in the characters in a movie... in your mind!

Then, when something happens to the carpet it feels as though it's happening to you. So you create an emotional disturbance in your consciousness called anger. The anger is of course suffering. If you want to be anger-free, fear-free, sorrow-free, then you will need to have a relationship of non-attachment with the carpet!

If you are 'non-attached' then, when the coffee lands, you will not get angry or upset in any way. You will not suffer. In that moment you are liberated from attachment to, and identification with, the carpet! You are liberated from making the mistake of losing your sense of self in an image of the carpet. You are no longer identifying your self with a carpet. So the next time a guest, plus coffee, plus gravity, inflicts a stain on your carpet you respond calmly and coolly. "No problem," you say. "Let's clean the carpet before the stain dries in", as you wander calmly towards the kitchen to get the carpet stain cleaning cloth... or something to that effect!

How to Care More

Whether it's a carpet, a position, a belief or another person that you are attached to, it's exactly the same mechanism and mistake as you lose your 'self' in what's on your mind! At which point most people jump up and shout, "But that means you need to be truly free, you need to be detached, from everything and everyone! Doesn't that mean you don't care". Yes to the first part. To be a truly free spirit there would be no attachment to anything or anyone whatsoever. Which is why truly free spirits are an extremely rare species!

No to the second part. Detachment or non-attachment, does not mean that you do not care. Neither is it a form of avoidance. It means the opposite. Non-attachment means you are then 'internally free', and therefore both available and able to be more caring. You are no longer busy losing your 'self' in a mental image and then mentally defending your attachment against any 'imagined' threat. You are no longer occupied with your emotions of frustration when someone doesn't act in the way you want, according to the image/idea you have created of them in your mind. You will naturally be more flexible, more available for others and therefore more caring. It means the energy you are able to give to others is calmer, clearer and likely to be more appropriate. You will not 'react' emotionally, thereby making your self suffer. You will be able to 'respond' more creatively and compassionately to the needs of others.

A Perfect Weather Day

We all tend to become a bit like a jumping Jack Flash as we keep losing our self in a thousand things/images that we create on the screen of our minds. Watch your self during the course of an average day or an average conversation. When you start to 'react emotionally' to anything or anyone, you will notice you are attached to an image of something or someone that's on your mind. When you complain about the weather you are attached to an image of what a perfect weather day this 'should be'. When you worry about losing something it's always because you are attached to the 'image' in your mind of the object you fear losing. When you worry about losing someone else, it's because you are attached to an image in your mind of them being there, with you and for you. You are dependent on them in order to feel OK in yourself. Detachment doesn't mean you don't see them, have fun with them, do things together, maybe even live with them! It just means you are no longer dependent on them for what you think and feel within your self.

Detachment or non-attachment means freedom. Any kind of attachment means you are trapped in the image of the object of attachment in your own mind. It's impossible to be happy and content, loving and joyful, unless you are free within your being. Hence the long line of sages and saints, mystics and gurus who have all expounded on the great mistake of attachment, and the necessity to cultivate a relationship of non-attachment with... everything!

At this point you may be tempted to attribute the suggestion of non- attachment to one particular spiritual or religious philosophy. Try not to do that, but instead see if it's true for you. True in your own personal experience.

The Two Trains Illusion

Here is another way to see it. Have you ever been sitting on a train in a station and there is another train alongside your train? Eventually your train starts to move and you are under the impression your journey has started. Then, after a few seconds, there is an announcement to say that your train will be departing in a few minutes. Suddenly you realize your train is still standing at the station and it's the other train that is moving.

So here you are, within your consciousness, looking at what's on your mind. There is a story moving across your mind and you believe that 'you' are moving in and with the story. Well you're not. That's an illusion, just like the train illusion. You are still. It's the images on your mind that are moving, which also means changing, just as in the cinema your body is sitting still but it's the projector and the images on the screen that are all moving and changing. As you play the movie in your mind you are affected by the story because you believe you are moving in and with the story. But in reality, you aren't. It's an illusion. It sometimes seems like a pleasant illusion, but it's still an illusion.

The truth is you are always still. Always in your soft and comfy inner seat within... YOU. But you fall under the illusion that you are moving along in a story, that you are acting in the story and contributing to the story, that you are changing in the story. The story is moving but you are not. As long as you stay in the illusion that you are moving there will be attachment to something in the story, and the ego will be born by identifying with the object of attachment. Then your contribution to the story will be distorted by attachment and ego, which, as we will see, will not be a loving and peaceful contribution, but fearful and angry.

This is why the practice of meditation, while cultivating self-awareness, is essentially an exercise in realizing your stillness. Paradoxically, to the rational mind at least, your contribution to life will be something of great beauty when you are free of the illusion that you change and you know your self as the still, unchanging self. You are stillness. That is why you are always 'still your self'... so to speak! In truth it is impossible to be anything other than your self. That means you never change. It means you may change identities just as the body changes clothes. But the self, the you, the being of consciousness that you always are, never changes. You just fall under the spell, under the illusion that you change.

PAUSE

Contemplate images and symbols of stillness. Don't get lost in them, but contemplate them, use them, to get a feeling for, an inner sense of, what it's like to be still. Use images and ideas from nature. Then allow your self to be image free and see if you can just be still. Try not to 'make' it happen but 'allow' your self to be still... be still... be still... be st...

Insight FIVE

How do you know you are in an EGO state?

All stress, suffering or sorrow, any form of unhappiness, means there is the presence of ego. You are not free. Free to roam the world perhaps, but not free in your being. You are attaching your 'self' to, and identifying with, an image or an idea of some 'thing' in your own mind. You are making a mistake. There is no 'thing' and no 'one' in the world 'out there', or in the world 'in here', that is you! Everything you have been told about your self (belief), about who you are, is not you! There is nothing material, including the sounds of physical words, or the deepest conceptual meanings of those words, that can define the reality of you.

But we are bewitched by the world, by the glamours of the world, by the media's projections, by all its material influences, into believing we can be, should be, have to be, will be, not just a body in the world, but 'somebody' in the world. In truth, however, we are just 'IN a body' that is in the material world.

The full realization of this is the ultimate enlightenment, the final freedom and the completion of the only 'real' journey we ever make, the journey into and out of forgetfulness.

That may sound dry and boring in theory. But the actuality of that free 'state of consciousness' is not. In that 'being free' state of awareness you fully enjoy being in this physical world. You know the 'joy of being' in the world. But that joy is yours, that joy is you! It is arising from within as you celebrate just being here. It's not a sourced or stimulated joy from anything in the world so it's not dependent on anything in the world.

It is a natural joyfulness that can only arise when you are not attached to, or identified with, anything or anyone in the world. As soon as you attach your self to anything or anyone then suffering, in the form of joylessness, is guaranteed. There are many 'excitements', which follow worldly stimulations. They are mistaken for joy, but they are not real joy, just temporary excitements. Unfortunately however, excitement is addictive! Like heroin is to the body and brain, so excitement is to the soul/self!

Building on Sand
The virus of the ego is a virus we all inherit. It is the inclination to build a sense of identity based on something or someone in the world. But this is the same as building a skyscraper on sand. There will be an inevitable collapse. In the context of the conscious being that I/you/we are, 'collapse' is code for stress and unhappiness, insecurity and resentment. This is why almost everyone, to some extent or other, is stressed and unhappy. Everyone catches the 'I am just a body' or 'I am somebody' virus! As long as you mistake your self for something that you are not, there must be an underlying dissatisfaction at best, extreme unhappiness at worst.

Even when we learn to be brave and smile our way through the day there will be many moments of miserableness behind our mask. Unless we have stopped trying to build on sand! Are you, in some way, continuously trying to build a sense of identity out of ideas, images and beliefs, and then have that identity recognized and celebrated by others? Do you seek to be affirmed by others in any way? Are you continuously trying to find your joy in the world, from the world? It is impossible. The suffering that follows the inevitable failure, and the disillusionment it creates, results in a growing sense of hopelessness and helplessness. Eventually depression!

We then try to mask those growing feelings, submerge those feelings, by using some form of stimulation with which to stimulate and 'excite' our self. From chocolate to bungee jumping, from television to celebrity watching, from shopping to drinking – these and a thousand other ways are used/consumed/indulged, in order to avoid dealing with the products of the ego which are the various forms of emotional suffering that we often call stress.

The Clash of Egos

The resulting 'internal' unhappiness finds many 'expressions' in the context of our relationships, such as criticizing, arguing, fighting and killing. Switch on the news and mostly you will see egos fighting egos, either verbally, politically or militarily, and in various other ways.

It's just people believing they are someone other than who they are - trying to impose their illusions about themselves onto others in order to have their illusions about themselves affirmed by others! They are trying to be somebody and be recognized by others as somebody significant! It's a popular dis – ease of consciousness often referred to LGS, i.e. Looking Good Syndrome! But we know not what we do, which means we don't understand how we are being driven by our own miscreation, by our own mistaken sense of self. When you see how the world is run by ego, how it's running on ego, locally and globally, the destiny of our world, of the species we call human beings in the world, becomes fairly obvious. Chaos awaits. On the other side of chaos there may be order. But in between is healing, which is messy!

As you become more aware, you will start to notice which of your behaviors are signs that you are asleep and that your sense of self, your identity, is lost in something you are not! Here are a few of the most common behavioral signs of ego's presence:

ARGUING means you are attached to, and identified with, a belief or beliefs, which usually includes the belief that 'I am right and you are wrong'. As soon as you realize you are not your beliefs you start to free your self from the source of suffering that underlies arguing. Sometimes we call this 'letting go'.

SHOUTING is a sign that you are attached to, and identified with, an image of what the other should have done but didn't, or an image of what they should not have done, but did! Shouting has an emotional driver called anger, and anger is suffering. Stop creating and identifying with an image/idea of someone else's behavior and that source of suffering is healed. Sometimes we call this 'letting be'!

RUNNING away is usually a sign you are attached to an idea or image of your self being unconfronted and unrevealed! You're in hiding! You are hiding something and you are attached to the idea of concealment. As soon as you stop, open up and be transparent then that source of suffering comes to an end. Sometimes we call this 'letting your self be seen!'

ENVYING is a signal that you are attached to an image of your self possessing and owning something that someone else has. That can range from a material possession to a position, from a reputation to a lifestyle. You have not yet realized that you are not an image of any thing, especially the image of an ideal lifestyle. You are you! When you free your self to be who you really are, which is no one possessing no thing, you will end the suffering that is envy. Sometimes we call this 'letting go and letting me... be me'!

MANIPULATING, which is a form of attempted controlling, is a sign that you are attached to, and identified with, an image of someone being or doing exactly what YOU want. As soon as you accept others as they are and as you find them, then the suffering that is frustration towards others, comes to an end. Sometimes we call this 'allowing'!

DEFENDING is usually a sign that you are attached to, and identified with, the image or the idea of 'my position' or 'my possession' with the emphasis on 'my'. When you perceive a threat to the position or possession you see it as a threat to you. The moment your realize you are not your position or your possession, then you stop seeing threats, you stop imagining future loss and the suffering known as fear is over. You are not a position or a possession. You are just you! Sometimes we call this 'letting everything come and go'.

CRITICIZING is an attack on another's creation. It could be their idea or their behavior that is triggering your habit of disapproval. It just means you are attached to your idea, your way, your ideals. Or you want to stop them getting ahead because you are attached to a picture of you being the frontrunner in the relationship. That's when you see their creation as a threat to you. So you fear and fight. You acclaim your superiority and attack with criticism to ensure their inferiority. All the while you are the embodiment of unhappiness, without realizing that you are the creator of your misery. Can you turn it around? When you embrace, encourage and empower the ideas and ways of others you will instantly notice you are empowering your self. You notice that true creativity is when you give your energy to others in ways that empower them. Being egoless then seems not only possible, but probably the only way to be real and build solid relationships. Sometimes we call this 'nurturing and nourishing'.

What's to Lose?

There are obviously many different behaviors that arise from the ego, behind which there is always an attachment to a mental image. In between the attachment/misidentification and the resulting behavior, is emotion. The most common emotion is fear. Fear is always the 'fear of loss'. Always the fear of losing something that you are attached to, in which you have trapped your own sense of self. This is why loss is personal and why fear is all pervasive in the world today!

The fear of losing what you identify with is really fear of losing your identity, which is a fear of losing your self, which is a fear of losing your life, which is a fear of death! The great big paradox however, is that you have already lost your identity, frequently, in some idea or image in your own mind. In fact most people spend most of their days, and indeed all of their lives, losing their identity as they lose themselves in many images and ideas in their own minds every minute of every day.

We grow up thinking this is normal, believing it's the way life is meant to be. This is why life itself can seem like one long 'near death' experience! Every time you attach to, and identify with, what you are not, in your own mind, it's as if you are trying to kill your 'self'! But you are not aware of it. In fact we all come to believe almost the opposite i.e. that life is about grabbing, attaching and building our sense of identity around what we believe we have got or will get! This is why, if you contemplate and see for your self how often you misidentify your self with something you are not you will eventually realize life is death and death is life. It's often called 'dying alive'. When you do let go of any attachment, anything that you are using to create a false identity, it feels like you are dying, but on the other side you will feel as if you have just started to live... for real!

Imagining your self 'letting go' then invokes a fear of losing the object of attachment upon which the self has become dependent. We imagine it's going to feel like a kind of death. In reality however, when what is let go has gone, and any residual craving has subsided, there is a new freedom. Letting go is then seen and felt to be more like liberation, which in turn restores an authentic inner happiness.

PAUSE

At the end of the day take five minutes and write down all the behaviors that you noticed your self creating through the day that indicate you are being driven by the ego? Behind each behavior what are you attached to in your own mind? Take a moment to imagine what it would be like to let go and what behavior would then emerge in that situation.

Have you ever created an illusion about your self and then tried to convince others of its reality in order to acquire their applause, their approval or their acceptance? When was the last time? What did you want others to see you as? How did you feel when they did or when they didn't?

This is the great trap we all tend to spring as we make our way through life. Once we are in the trap we struggle with what has come to be known as huge self-esteem and self-worth issues. So huge they now have their own industry! We don't realize we are trying to find our worth in the one place it can never exist, in the words and behaviors of others. The actor tries to find it in their audience, the singer tries to find in their record sales, the politician tries to find it in votes, we all, at some stage will try to find it in our family, boss or work colleagues. But it's just not 'there'. It's always 'here', within our self. It's just that to know it we will need to stop searching for it!

Insight SIX

Where does it all begin and when will it all end?

It all starts with our physical body. It's the first attachment and the first thing we mistakenly identify with. We learn to believe we are our body. We look in a mirror and see an image of our body. We then bring that image into our mind, memorize it, and build our sense of identity from it and around it. Then, depending on the nature and extent of our conditioning, which will depend on a number of factors like parents and culture, we might spend the rest of our life worried about our 'body image'. Most of us will become 'appearance conscious', which is often mistakenly called being self-conscious. But in truth, it's not 'self' conscious, it's 'body' conscious. Some will spend large amounts of money nipping, tucking, slimming, trimming, strengthening, scraping, scrubbing and doing just about everything to their body in order to make what they misguidedly believe is their 'self' better looking!

For others, their identity and therefore their ego, will become more about their individual reputation in the eyes of others in the world, or more about recognized achievements around the world, or just the quantity and size of their acquisitions from the world. All these misidentifications are sustained by a desire to be seen to 'be somebody' in the eyes of others!

It becomes obvious that if we are to be free, if we are to be our self again, if we are to liberate our self from the habit of attachment and misidentification, if we are to stop creating our own unhappiness, it would help if we could stop trying to be what we are not! That would be made easier if we could be who we really are. Which is, in essence, no one!

However, considering our self to be 'no one' can seem a little weird at best and totally alien at worst. So it helps to use another word to describe the being that we are. Spirit, soul, consciousness, authentic self, all do the job! At least until the actual realization that 'I am no one' is realized for real!

Energy of Life

It starts with 'considering' your self as such, then, as you meditate on that 'information', as you contemplate its implications, as you open and look with your inner eye in the direction in which that insight points, gradually you start to remember and realize for yourself, that's what you really are. No one! Just the essential 'energy of life' that brings form to life!

Slowly, but surely, you will start to notice and realize for your self the mistake of attaching your self to anything, the mistake of considering your self to be just a body, the mistake of attempting to 'create' an identity in the world and building your self-belief upon it. That's not to say you walk through the world in a zombie like state uttering. "I am no one... really!" Men in white coats may follow! That's not to say you just sit down and give up on life in a state of hopelessness and helplessness. Those are signs of depression not liberation.

All Asleep!

Once you realize the deepest habit within the consciousness of just about everyone around you is to create a false identity, it changes almost everything. You realize everyone else is asleep too! Once you realize everyone's suffering/stress is self-made simply because of their ego, it changes your attitude to everyone. It awakens within you a new understanding and a genuine compassion. It shapes a new attitude towards the world and empowers you to be an enabling presence for others. Your realization of your spiritual essence and your liberation from the habit of creating an ego becomes both an example and an enlightening presence for those still in the dark.

Language of Labels

The realization of your authentic self brings with it an awareness that life itself is 'the game' and the game of life invites you to play! Just being here means you have already accepted the invitation. So you develop ways to playfully 'play' the game of life as you find it. You still pay your bills and drive your car and go to work, but with a completely different perspective and attitude. You speak the international language of labels because that's the language everyone else is speaking in their sleepiness. You may even look and sound like you are still asleep, still as unaware as everyone else. But in the reality of your consciousness you are awake and aware of your self as a free being, attached to no one and no thing! You no longer speak and act to sustain a false self, you no longer seek to gain approval for what you want others to see you as, you no longer defend an ego. In fact you don't need to defend anything anymore!

You are now able to be your true self, which wants nothing from others and yet is available for others. You are now secure in your self because you know your self as you really are. As you 'live from' this inner reality you are calm and caring, loveful and light-hearted, contented and compassionate, because this is the natural nature of being your true self, which is no one!

As you live and breathe, talk and walk, from this true sense of self, it will be noticed by others. Perhaps it may arouse their curiosity. When it does you are able to recognize their curiosity as an opportunity to share with them what you have realized for your self.

And so, as one candle ignites another, as one flame passes on its fire, so you may spark a moment of 'I too am no one' enlightenment in another. But usually only when you least intend it!

This process of re-awakening, if self-realization, doesn't happen all at once. It tends to be gradual. It can feel like three steps forward and two steps back, as you habitually re-energize old false identities that you thought had gone for good, until the habit has gone. Sometimes just reading about it all in this context can make the process, the journey, 'seem' long and laborious and hard. So patience is your mantra and perseverance is your watchword!

Practice Patiently but Persistently

But you can start with little things. Experiment with non-attachment to the less significant things in your life. Experiment with letting go, with releasing! This will happen naturally within you when you practice and develop the ability to pull back from what's on your mind and recognize there is you, there is your mind and there is what is on your mind. The more you practice this the more your thoughts, in the form of those ideas, images, concepts, which are all different kinds of memories, start to slow and eventually stop coming to mind! Eventually! Then you will find you're thinking only what is necessary in response to what is in front of you in the moment.

You will start to 'lighten up', as they say, and the face you wore in order to convince others you were OK and happy, which was previously either a little forced or a bit temporary, will start to become real and natural. Ever since our childhood we have been attaching and misidentifying and creating the many faces of ego. The habit is deep. We have become so familiar with our various ego generated personas we will not want to give them up so easily, even when our continual insecurity, perhaps frequent rage, perhaps depression, all conspire to send us the message that it's time to do this inner work.

Your Invitation to a Fancy Dress Party

Here is another way to perceive and meet the challenge of waking up and staying awake to who you are as no one!   Go to the theatre and watch a one man or woman show. Notice how they may play as many as six different parts. They adopt six different personas or identities. After each one they drop that persona, they dissolve the ego of that character, and then create and adopt the next one. Then at the end of the evening they drop them all and they go home and be themselves. They return to being the persona that was prior to playing all the different characters. If they don't, therapy is not far away!

Similarly we start to recognize the masks that we create and wear, the different faces of our own ego. We notice we have been putting on some kind of performance in order to sustain them. This takes energy and is tiring, not to mention the emotional content that comes with each false persona. Can you drop all the persona, take off all the masks, and just be your self? Be simple, be calm, be attentive, be aware, be free.

Life is like a fancy dress party! Everyone learns to dress themselves up. Not in clothing but in the images and ideas, concepts and beliefs about their 'self'. Take off your fancy dress. Strip your self naked. There is nothing more liberating than just being... me! Can you see?

PAUSE

Sit quietly. Close your eyes. Imagine your body has disappeared but you are still here. Now imagine your self being free of all responsibilities and obligations. Imagine you are free to say and do anything. You don't need anything from anyone. You don't have to keep up any appearances whatsoever.

Insight SEVEN

What would life be like in an egoless world?

Many people believe life would be boring without all the emotional dramas that our ego creates in order to get some attention and affirmation. All manufactured entertainment is, after all, simply ego's games given a safe and glamorized context for our emotional indulgence. Yet, as we have seen, it's only when you are without ego that you can be a truly free and peaceful spirit. We have moments, usually in our younger years, when we taste such an inner freedom, and with it comes a joyfulness, an authentic happiness, that is without opposite. Any form of attachment kills our 'freedom of spirit' as we become 'trapped in' the objects of attachment or more accurately in the images of the objects of attachment in our minds. When you have no ego you have no need to attempt to establish a sense of who you are in the minds of others. You don't need anyone else to affirm you, to accept you, to approve of you. All those needy habits, the anxiety that accompanies them, and the moods that arise from them, disappear. The mental and emotional suffering that results from NOT getting the approval, acceptance and acknowledgement of others is gone.

When you practice detaching i.e. building relationships based on non-attachment, you will notice your true underlying nature beginning to shine through from the heart of your own being. The different forms of the emotion we call fear, that must arise when we mistakenly equate detachment with loss, no longer occur.

For that is all fear is, the 'imagined' loss of something we are attached to in our own minds. If you can realize NOW that you have nothing to lose because nothing is ever 'mine', then fear becomes impossible.

An egoless world would therefore look like a world that had no fear and therefore no conflict. There would be no 'us and them', no mine and yours, no borders or barriers to separate us from each other. No urge to defend, no intolerance of others. No one would be stressed by anything or anyone. No one would fear loss or feel sadness after loss of any kind because a universal truth would have 'kicked in' – the truth that nothing and no one was ever 'mine' in the first place.

A Mutual Creation

There would be a *harmony* based on mutual respect; a *sharing* based on a mutual appreciation of each other's presence; a perception of *abundance* based on a mutual acknowledgment of plenty; a *celebration* of each others presence based on a mutual understanding that each one of us is a source of love and joy in the world. It would be a jointly created paradise, as each one would bring the beauty of their spirit into the world in their own unique ways.

Boring? Only for those addicted to their emotional dramas; only for those who are dependent on some form of violence to feel some sense of power in their life; only for those who are attached to something or someone as they use the idea of that thing, or the image of that person, to define themselves; only for those dependent on something in the world for what they mistakenly believe is responsible for their personal happiness. So that's just about everyone then!

There's an old saying; 'we don't budge until it hurts'. Which means we don't change, we won't change our ways, until we 'have to' change, until we are suffering so intensely that we consciously seek relief from the emotional pain. Up until that point we tolerate our suffering and will even use it as another form of false identity. So who knows how long we will need to wait till enough people suffer enough to say, "No more, I can tolerate this suffering, this unhappiness, no more, there must be another way". Until then we will probably see those who are suffering continue to project their suffering onto others who are already suffering! Such is the power of presence of the ego within the consciousness of just about every human being. In the meantime we each have the same choice: to liberate our self from our own emotional suffering by dissolving the ego, or continue to make our self stressed and frequently unhappy.

Return to the Center

Watch for the ego at work in others. Not out of desire to judge them or find fault in them, but as an exercise in raising your awareness of the presence of ego behind many of your own behaviors. Every time you spot someone acting or reacting from ego ask your self if you say or do the same. If you do then hunt down what you are attached to internally. Can you see the idea or image in your mind that you have lost your self in? Gradually you will start to notice the mental image you are attached to and how you use to manufacture a false sense of self. Gradually you will withdraw your energy from your mental images and return to the center of... you! As you do, all the habitual false identities will start to die of natural causes! Your inner peace will return. You will feel the rusty gates of your true heart squeaking and squealing as they re-open after a long time shut, metaphorically speaking! Then, when you are naked, stripped clean of all illusory ideas about your self, when you know that you are 'no one', you will smile the smile of enlightenment as you realize the true meaning of that old saying... 'heaven is within'.

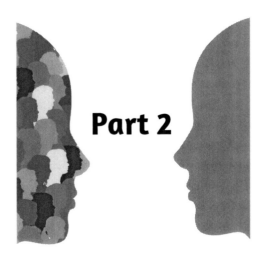

Part 2

The EGO at Work

How the ego runs the world!

It's not long after we arrive in this life that we are encouraged to start thinking, "What am I going to do with my life?" That soon becomes, "What am I going to do 'in life'?" Before we know it many of us will start generating our ambitions and visualizing future achievements. Possible vocations are sifted, professional destinies are discussed and aspirations to follow in the footsteps of another are often born! For some, usually the 'creatives', the merits of the maverick lifestyle are perceived as the only way to 'do life'. For most, with their decision made, it's off to higher education and out into the world of work and a career that is applauded by family and friends.

During the whole process, whatever direction it takes, what we don't notice is the quiet corruption of our consciousness. We don't notice that in seeking a stable and fruitful career or vocational path, we are also seeking a future identity. Perhaps the most common mistake we all learn to make is to identify with what we do. When you believe that you are your position or your profession, or even your trade, you are creating a belief that you are what you do. But it's not true. What you do is not what you are. Yet we look forward to telling others about what we do, believing they will see that as... 'me'!

We proudly hand over our response to the, "What do you do?", question at the party, either in words or on our card. Without realizing that our self-definition at that moment is, or will be, a major source of fear that we will come to know as insecurity. That's the problem with any false identity, it's always based on something that is not secure, not fixed, not unchanging, not unattackable.

If you base your sense of self on what you do it will generate the most common forms of fear: insecurity and anxiety. That's a fact that you can test and verify for your self. That fear will then interfere with everything in life from the way you work, the decisions that you make, to the relationships you build, or not build, as the case may be.

That's why the mistake of identifying with what we do and the resultant insecurity may well run our entire life. It does for some, such as those who are married to their desk or their phone or their workshop. It's this same mistake that runs the world, as it expands itself into the consciousness of just about everyone with a 'job'. Before we explore some of the precise 'doings' i.e. professions and positions that mostly run our 'beings' within the world, let's unpack some of the effects on our day-to-day lives. When you believe you are, and therefore identify with, what you do it creates the following conditions within your consciousness. These then become features of your personality that are then expressed in the way you live.

Vulnerable to Criticism

When you believe you are what you do the slightest criticism towards what you do will be taken personally. You will feel deflated as you believe you have lost your prestige in the eyes of others. That is likely to turn into a 'how dare they say that about me' resentment and a projection of that pain onto others. But it wasn't 'about me', it was about what 'me did'! Two different things!

Achievement is Rewarded

Most professions and vocations require sustaining through the achievement of targets, goals or levels of quality. This ensures a goal and reward driven life. The ability to be and live in the moment is easily lost, as energy and effort is continuously focused on achieving future goals and then 'worrying about' what will happen and how you will feel if you don't. Only achievement is celebrated and the ability to live life itself as a celebration, which basically means being choicefully happy every day, is diminished if not eliminated.

Security is Externalized

When you identify with what you do it means you will desire the recognition of others in order to feel you are worthy. Your inner sense of security will be dependent on others feedback. You may not notice that, in your sleepiness, you are actually creating feelings of insecurity by becoming dependent on others feedback for your security!

Competition is Encouraged

Those seeking any position in almost all professional arenas will find themselves competing for the position and the obvious rewards for 'winning' it. This engenders a mindset of win/lose, of 'to the victor the spoils'. In some it will result in a more ruthless form of 'it doesn't matter how you win, just win'. Yes there will be moments of 'victory happiness' known as euphoria based on winning, but such occasional 'highs' will be like punctuation marks in a long sentence of many lows.

Selfishness is Valued

The very idea that a position can be threatened or lost is guaranteed to engender the mindset of self-protection against the perceived manoeuvers and games of others. This tends to result in a 'look after number ONE philosophy', which is basically just a form of selfishness. It is to act against the very nature of being human. The heart becomes closed around the attachment, which is the position. The self limits itself as it sees itself only according to position and title. This creates a small sense of self. To make one's self small and closed is to sabotage one's true nature, which is open and unlimited. Unhappiness must ensue.

Desire is Cultivated

All of the above combine to fuel the growth of personal desire; desire for recognition, reward, affirmation, security and success in the eyes of others. These are self-serving desires and will ultimately tend to result in the alienation of others. Yet it's only in the context of our relationships that life can work. It's 'relationship' that gives us the opportunity to give freely of our self. Only in such moments can we come to know the beauty, richness and limitlessness of our own being. Paradox!

Vision is Narrowed

When we believe we are what we do, when we define our self by our position or profession, we create a narrow vision of life itself and how life should be lived. It becomes hard to see the bigger picture; the bigger, longer, wider view of, well, everything. This stunts our ability to cultivate the insight and foresight required to make wise decisions and choices.

And so, to the world! How does misidentification with what 'I do', one of many faces of the ego, get to run the world.

The Banker's World

See the banker who believes 'Banker is who and what I am'. His sense of identity is built around the idea and image of 'I am a Banker'. This means he gets to play with material wealth. He gets to create the systems within which money is managed. He handles what is the basis of most people's sense of financial security. What does the ego (the self mistaking itself for the idea/image of Banker) do? It serves itself. It creates thoughts, decisions and actions to sustain the image/idea/position of Banker. It makes sure 'I am going to survive as a Banker'. How? One way is to create and manipulate a monetary 'system' that ensures the financial wealth of many, flows to the few, which is basically how the monetary system now operates.

However the human being who believes they are a 'Banker' is not to blame for the systematic inequality of financial wealth distribution. Their actions are the result of the inherited beliefs that banking is the way to live your life, be a banker and be a successful banker, make banker your job and therefore your identity. This conditioning of a human being to identify with Banker has implications for all of us. What starts as, "I am here to provide you with a banking service for you and your money", eventually becomes "I am a Banker and it's my job to make a profit for me/us from your money". The person who believes they are a banker and who therefore exploits their 'public service position' for personal gain is not a bad person, they are just asleep. But they are not aware they are asleep. The 'ego' of I am a Banker becomes powerful and this same shift from 'service to survival', from public service to self service/survival, can be found in many other areas of professional life. The ego is at work.

The Politician's World

See the Politician who is attached to, and identified with, the belief that Politician is who and what I am. Fear of losing power and position will ensure they compromise their communication and relationships with others, especially those whom they represent. They will invent and play many types of political games in order to survive as a Politician and hold on to their power. They will even lie to those who would follow them in order to maintain their identity based on what they do. When people who believe 'I am a Politician' start to serve themselves they are not bad human beings, just asleep! But they are not aware they are asleep. The ego is a form of sleep!

The Scientist's World

Watch many scientists who believe 'I am a Scientist' and this is 'my position' which gives me 'my power'. This attachment to, and identification with, what they do will eventually ensure that some, perhaps many, scientists will compromise their own integrity and betray our trust. Some will likely find themselves being used by vested interests to ensure specific results of future research. Many will become dependent on 'research funds' from sources to whom they will consequently pander. Some may obfuscate, manipulate and falsify research. Others will 'get into bed' with corporations and politicians in order to serve their agenda at the cost of public health; all with the aim of protecting their sense of self as 'Scientist'. But they are not to blame. They are not bad people. Just asleep! They simply suffer from a dis-ease called ego, which will ensure they create insecurity in the form of fear and that fear will make them do and say strange and inaccurate things, as it does with us all at some point in our lives. In the laboratory of our consciousness we can watch the ego at work!

The Corporate Executive's World

The senior manager, the director, the chairman, all share the same sense of identity around 'Corporate Executive'. Their position and power give them the opportunity to seemingly have power over the lives of many working people below. While they may be somewhat responsible for a community of human beings known as 'staff' their identification with 'I am the Manager' or 'I am the Director' will ensure many of them will dabble in the art of manipulation and even exploitation. They will see their task is to make profit. Their position and power will be dependent on profit-making. So their insecurity will likely one day ensure that they run the company not for the benefit of anyone else but for themselves and the preservation of their position, which is the preservation of their ego, their identity based on position and power. They are not to blame. It's the ego that goes to work! They are asleep at their desk believing they are awake!

The Environmentalist's World

Yet, even though it's the ego of some of the people serving the four previous and many other 'professions' that are messing up the world at all levels, the protesting environmentalist, the activist, the resistor, is also suffering from their own ego based on the idea 'I am a world saver/changer'. Or something similar! Their fear for the future of the world means they are attached to an image of an ideal world, their version of that ideal world. That attachment, which 'they' would probably call a sensible and fair aspiration, will be responsible for their fears and anxieties, their angers and frustrations. These emotions will either lead to violence at worst or an ongoing resistance at best.

They will not therefore be able to access and use the wisdom required to free themselves from their own ego. This wisdom would guide them to sit and creatively influence others, as opposed to trying to control them. This wisdom would show them that any resistance towards anyone who mistakes themselves for any of the previous four positions and professions, will only generate resistance in return! Egos against egos, only has one outcome, further conflict, and an even deeper attachment to, and further entrenchment of, their positions.

Enlightened Engagement

So what can we do when we recognize that it's just egos that are running the world. It's obvious we cannot change others. This wisdom we know. But we can influence. We can lead. But only by example and through a more enlightened level of engagement. All we can do is re-awaken our self to our true self and nature. Only then can we show others, share with others, occasionally point out to others, with the insight of our own realizations, how they are making themselves both fearful and unhappy.

To many, this may sound naïve. It may sound like a fools approach to creating a better world. However, any other way that involves the emotions of fear or anger or resentment only adds to the suffering and darkness in the world. All resistance is based on fear and anger. All 'resistance movements' are built on fear and anger and therefore their own versions of ego. This is why the 'resistance approach' to creating a better future doesn't work.

Acceptance of the other does. Acknowledgement and appreciation of the other does. Understanding the other does. Listening to the other does. But it's not possible to bring these intentions and behaviors to the conversation until the ego is out of the way. It has to be dissolved first. That's why what's IN the way IS the way. But whisper it quietly to the banker, the scientist, the politician and you know who!

Perhaps one of the unwisest strategies is waiting for others to change their attitude and behavior. It's likely to be a very long wait!

Some say it's too late to change the world, too late for us to change what we are doing to the natural world. Others say we need to 'be the change we want to see in the world'. But perhaps the deepest wisdom comes from the realization that whatever state the world is in, whatever is happening in the world, is exactly the way things are meant to be. It's in the plan, if there is such a thing. It's this ability to accept and embrace the way things are that signifies an end to the resistance and resentment of the ego, which only alienates others. It's this perception that all is well, even when apparently it isn't, that creates the space in which we can connect and communicate with each other peacefully and creatively about the best ways forward.

But that kind of mindset is not easy, simply because our deepest habit is attachment, ego and the consequent fears. And fear has no patience, no capacity to listen and be co-creative, no ability to speak from a place of acceptance and appreciation of the other. And so it is that the ego runs the world and will likely run the world until the message from the world becomes loud enough or drastic enough to say 'enough'! That will likely be when we have no choice but to face the fact that we are all suffering from the same basic illusions. And then choose to awaken!

Part 3

Emotions at Play

Seven signposts into how
your emotions get IN the Way

First IN Sight

What is emotion exactly?

All emotions arise from the ego. Emotion is the price you pay today for your attachments yesterday. This is almost equally as challenging for most of us to see and understand as the creation of ego itself. That's because we tend to become both addicted to, and exhausted by, our emotions.

It's not easy to untangle our *emotions* from our *feelings*. The ideas and meanings of both are easily mixed in any conversation that is a mutual attempt to understand emotions and feelings! Once again an absence of emotional learning in our formal education or in our upbringing didn't help. Some languages don't even have two separate words so there is much confusion and many different descriptions of emotion. In one sense no one has the correct description, there is no single right understanding. There is therefore no substitute for exploring and feeling and seeing and naming and articulating for oneself. As you do you will find your own understanding of the cause and the nature of 'emotion' shifting as your clarity increases.

That means being extremely attentive to what is going on within your consciousness, where all emotion has its origin. Then learning to name the emotions that you create within your consciousness. Then, looking underneath the 'emotion' that you 'feel' to see the cause, to see how and why you created the 'emotion that you are feeling' in the first place. All of that requires the continuous and conscious cultivation of self-awareness (not self-consciousness or self-obsession) and a genuine interest to understand why you feel what you feel. This kind of self-understanding is both the big hole in our education and the missing level of guidance from our parents. They knew not that they knew not!

The Downward Causation of Emotion

One of the reasons we find it hard to discern the origins of our emotions is we don't really register our emotions until the energy of the emotion has an effect on some part of our body. Then we just say things like, "I feel nervous", as we hold our stomach, or "I feel angry", as we clench our fist and perhaps our teeth, or "I feel tense", after our whole body has stiffened up. We don't notice that the energy that is having such an effect on different areas of our body originates within our consciousness, from within our 'self'. It's a 'downward causation' from our consciousness to our body. It ripples down from the spiritual energy that we are, from our mind, to our body.

One definition of emotion (which is not carved in stone) also contains the mechanism by which you may start to see how you create your emotions.

Emotion is the disturbance of the energy of your consciousness (your 'self') when the object of attachment is damaged, threatened, moved or lost!

We all know a moment when we became emotionally disturbed, which basically means anything from 'mildly to extremely unhappy', about something or towards someone. It normally occurs when someone does not do, say or be what you want, and then you become upset. Such as: when property is damaged; when you are on the end of someone's insult; when someone lies to you; when you get feedback that others are gossiping about you. These are just a few of the numerous moments when most of us tend to develop the habit of 'reacting emotionally'. It's a crude misuse of our energy, which signifies we have lost control of our consciousness, of our self, and an 'emotional flaring' has taken over.

Let's stay, for a moment, with the example of someone not doing what I WANT or doing what I DON'T WANT! Whenever you 'react' emotionally towards another there is a disturbance that you create in your consciousness. 'They' are not responsible for your emotional disturbance. They are just doing what they are doing, or not, as the case may be! Seeing and accepting total responsibility for all your emotional disturbances is the first step in liberating your self from your self-inflicted suffering!

Attachment is the Culprit

While such disturbances are 'emotions being created' in consciousness, they all differ to some degree. Some are called frustration or sadness or sorrowfulness or hopelessness or anxiety or resentment - the list is almost endless. (see the list of emotions and their common causes on pages 117 to 121). This is because the 'object of attachment', which is the mental image of the other person doing exactly what you want, which you have created 'in here' in your own mind as an expectation, is damaged by the reality of the person 'out there' not doing it!

If you were not attached to that image, and did not lose your sense of self in the image of the other doing what 'I WANT' then, when the other person failed to do what you wanted, or expected, or preferred, you would not distort the energy of your consciousness into frustration/anger. You would not have become 'emotional'. You would not suffer. You would not have whipped up the energy of your consciousness into the emotion (energy in motion) of anger or one of anger's many versions. You would more likely have asked them 'why' they hadn't done what you expected, in a genuine enquiry to understand why the other was either not able, or didn't want to, or could not, do what they said they would.

Have you ever lost your car keys? Notice the 'disturbance' originating in your consciousness called tension. And how the tension intensifies the longer the keys are missing. So there is a disturbance in your consciousness called 'tension' because the object of 'attachment' has been lost. Or it could be that an image of you arriving at some destination on time is being threatened by the absence of a set of car keys! Then, as soon as you find your keys, the tension dissolves instantly and you are free from that emotion. The suffering instantly subsides. Some people, when they lose their keys, do not suffer. They don't create the emotions we call anxiety and tension. They stop, sit down, relax, contemplate patiently and knowingly as they ask themselves, "Now the keys are around here somewhere, I'll see them in a moment. Where was the last time I saw them? Where might they have fallen?" In other words no tension, no disturbance, no suffering... no emotion! In effect, they become 'centered' in a state of calmness, from which a memory of where the keys were last seen can arise unclouded and unobstructed by any... emotion!

Boss Approval

The train is late. You are standing worriedly on the platform. You might miss the meeting. It's an important meeting, which the boss said you must not miss. So you create a disturbance in your consciousness called fear. Why? Because you are attached to the image of being on time and being approved of by your boss for being punctually present for the meeting. Your 'sense of self' is based on an image of being a punctual person and dependent on the idea of consistently acquiring 'boss approval'. Whereas the person next to you on the platform, also late for their meeting, is light and carefree. They know they have no control over the speed of the train. They are not dependent on the approval of others, as they know their own value. Internally they are free. No attachment to, and no identification with, a mental image, equals no ego, equals no emotion, equals no fear, equals no panic, equals no self-created suffering, equals no damage to personal happiness!

Farewell to Mum!

Your mother dies. You cry as you create the emotion of sorrow. Why? Isn't that natural? Well yes, and no. Most people learn to 'believe' it's natural to grieve, to create the emotions of sorrowfulness. But when you do you are suffering. You are the creator of the suffering, not your mother or her death. The physical equivalent might be likened to sticking a knife in your leg. But we don't do that and call it natural! So why the mental/emotional suffering? Because you are attached to, and identified with, the image, the idea, the memory, of 'my mother'. But how can you not be? Well some aren't. In fact, in some cultures they don't cry at the passing of another, even a family member, they celebrate. That's because they have a different vision of the other and relationship with the other, including mother! It's sometimes because they don't believe a death is a loss, an ending, but a gateway to the start of a new adventure.

Your Attached One!

It doesn't matter too much what your understanding or philosophy is around death at this moment. What is useful to recognize/realize is that even when a so-called 'loved one' passes on, it's still you that makes your self suffer, it's not their passing, it's not the event. The object of attachment (your mother) has 'apparently' been lost, so you create a disturbance in your consciousness, a distortion in your being, called sorrow. In truth, if you do create sorrow it means your mother wasn't really your 'loved one', she was really your 'attached one'! You were so attached to the image of your mother being with you 'in here', that when the physical form has gone from 'out there' in your life, you created and felt the sorrow that follows when you believe you have lost someone. But if you were not attached to your mother, if perhaps you saw her, like your self, as a spiritual being on her journey, and not only as MY mother, you would not suffer...so much! If you saw how you were able to share some precious time and co-create special moments together, until the inevitable moment came in which to go your separate ways, you would more likely generate appreciation (which is love) for her, and you would not suffer. You would not be so attached, so dependent, so there would be much less and maybe even no sorrow, no suffering. Easy theory! But is it possible? Some say: "Yes, why not!" Most say: "You have to be kidding!" Neither is right or wrong. What say you? Contemplate it and see for your self. If you create sorrow it means you 'believe' you have lost something/someone, which means you 'believe' that you possessed something/someone. Do you, can you, ever possess anyone?

From a purely spiritual point of view mother/father are just roles that the soul/spirit may play during a lifetime. It's not what they are, it's not what the 'I' that says 'I am' is! But that's not an easy realization until we are fully aware of the reality of our own spiritual identity, which is no identity!

Free Floating Anxiety!
So this is why and how ALL emotion, all disturbances within consciousness, arise from attachment, from the self losing itself in the image of the object of attachment on the screen of the mind. It all happens in our minds. Hence the truth in the saying; 'it's all in the mind'. Well nearly all! That's also why we don't usually cry when a thousand other people's mothers pass away every day, as they do! All mental/emotional suffering comes from the ego, from the attachment to and identification with, an image, idea, memory,

concept or belief appearing in our own minds. The appearance of, the attachment to, and the misidentification with, any particular mental image can last for anything from a few seconds, to many years, to a lifetime. In the case of attachment to other people it's usually a very long time!

Our days are full of many such moments as we habitually recreate a variety of images and ideas in our minds, then attach our self to each, for various lengths of time. Hence the free floating anxiety (fear) that many of us seem to create and feel almost continuously as we dance across all our attachments in our own minds throughout each and every day! The images/ideas themselves can be gross, as in clear mental pictures of things and people, or they can be extremely subtle, as in subconscious, previously assimilated beliefs or deep memories.

Double Trouble!

It's easy to avoid your emotions, to push them aside in favor of feeling something better. It's easy to take something, consume something, press a button on the TV remote or even press someone else's buttons, in order to not feel the emotion that is arising within you for whatever reason. But that only stores up double trouble for later. Best to look squarely at the emotion, fully acknowledge its discomfort and then... name it! As you do, two things happen. First, you are naturally detaching from the emotion. In other words you are withdrawing the life-giving energy of your consciousness, so the emotion must subside and die. All emotion dies under observation.

Second, you will start to develop your 'emotional literacy'. Just as those who cannot read tend to remain uneducated and therefore somewhat naïve about many areas of life, so too, if you cannot read your own emotions you will likely remain naïve regarding how and where and why you become attached and thereby lose your spiritual power. Learning to recognize and read your own emotional states then becomes the foundation for your ability to recognize and empathize with others' emotional states.

What About Love and Happiness

At this point many do say, or ask, isn't love also an emotion, isn't happiness also an emotion? Which tends to confirm our confusion around emotions. Take a moment to reflect and you may begin to see that love and happiness are states of being, free of any emotional disturbance. They are states that are only possible to create, to 'be in', when there is no attachment and therefore no emotional disturbance. That is definitely not easy to see, as most of us have learned that love and attachment come together, that they are one and the same.

When you are being loving you cannot be attached to anything. If you are then fear arises, which is the opposite of love. When you are loving you are not emotional. There is no disturbance in your consciousness, only the natural free flow of the energy of you to the other. When you are content, which is the deepest form of happiness, you are not disturbed by emotion. You are not 'emotional'. You are naturally extending the energy of 'you', in a state of contentment, out into the world of your relationships. If you are emotional then it's not true love, you're busy with your self, you're busy feeling your own emotions. It's not authentic happiness if there is any emotion. Emotion always signals agitation and more often discontentment. And that can never be happiness.

PAUSE

Find a recent real life situation where you became very sad. Re-run it in your mind as if you are watching a movie. Contemplate it. See if you can see what you were attached to in your mind during and after that/those scenes. What do you believe has been lost? What is the image in your mind you are holding onto and losing your self in?

Second ᘰᘰ IN Sight

What is feeling and what's the difference between our emotions and feelings?

When asked, "Who does your thinking?" Most people reply, "I do!" Obviously. When asked, "Who chooses or decides what you think about?" Again, most people say, "I do", of course! But when asked, "Who does your feeling?" Most people look a little perplexed. They are unsure. Some for a few moments, others for many moments! There is almost no point in asking who 'chooses' your feelings, as most people, if they think about it for long enough, seem utterly confused. This is usually because we have all learned to believe that ALL that we feel comes from 'outside in'. We believe other people and events are responsible for our feelings. That means we have not yet learned to choose and create our feelings in the same way that we might consciously choose and create our thoughts.

So what is a feeling exactly, and why are we so incapable of choosing what we feel? There is one simple dictionary definition.

Feeling is Perception by Touch

At a physical level we perceive the texture and the quality of the cloth of a dress or suit by *touching* it. We *feel* it by using our physical sense of *touch*. This is a 'physical feeling', using our physical senses. Obviously!

When someone says something and explains the logic of what they are saying, a little voice in our head probably whispers 'yes I see that, I perceive that', which is a way of saying, I 'feel' the logic of that.

This is feeling at a *rational level*. On another occasion when someone just makes a statement without any explanation or logic, our little voice also sometimes says 'yes, I see that, that feels right, I don't know why, I don't see any logic, but it just feels right!' In such instances we are 'feeling' at a deeper level, the *intuitive level*.

So we can touch, see, perceive, feel, at a rational level and we can see, perceive, touch, feel, at an intuitive level. These are what you might call 'subtle feelings'.

The Subtler Flavors

But the deepest, most subtle 'feelings' are spiritual. Many of us have known someone whose 'presence' we feel. We don't have to see them but they can be in the house and we feel their energy. Sometimes they can be in another building, sometimes far away, and we feel their energy. These are the subtlest of feelings. Some of us are more sensitive to such feelings than others. It's a bit like spicy food. If you eat hot and spicy food regularly you will likely lose some of your sensitivity to the subtler flavors of some foods. So it is with feeling. If you have indulged intensely in physical sensations over a period of time then your ability to feel the subtler energies of the spiritual emanations of others will be diminished. And that's exactly what we have all being doing - indulging in the intensity of physical stimulation to such an extent that many of us grow up believing feelings are only physical sensations. We have mostly lost our capacity to sense and feel the subtle energy, the spiritual energy that emanates from the consciousness of others.

But the deepest feeling you can choose to have is when you bring your attention and awareness inwards to your self. In the space of a few seconds you can create a state of inner peace and you will 'feel peace'. In a matter of seconds you can create a state of lovefulness towards someone, or towards the world, and 'feel that love' as it emanates outwards from your self. That's really what we are all searching for IN the world: to feel peace and love. Yet it is always accessible at all times, in all situations, in an instant, within our self. All we have to do is choose to create and give that state of consciousness and then we will 'feel it'! We all know from experience it's in the giving that we feel it.

Overpowered by Belief

So why can't you? The primary reason is our old friend the ego. You are attached to and overpowered by the belief that other people and circumstances 'make you feel' what you feel. So you are always on the lookout to 'get' something to 'make you feel'. When you don't get what you want, i.e. what you are already attached to in your mind, you create an emotional reaction. When you become emotional it's the emotion that gets IN the way. It sabotages your ability to choose and create your state of consciousness and therefore your feelings! Emotion is always the result of attachment. So it's the attachment to an image/idea in our mind (of what I WANT/HAVE) that gets IN the way. Any idea/image in your mind that YOU attach your SELF to then defines your sense of identity and therefore the ego is born... again! So it's the ego that's IN the way!

That last paragraph is the essence of this book and the biggest clue in the great *How to Be Free and Happy* puzzle that we all try to solve!

Notice that whenever you are emotional it's impossible to choose your feelings! Until the emotion dies, as all emotions eventually do, only then can you choose what you will feel! But that is not so easy, as most of us have been taught that the only way to feel is to emote! Many of us have been taught that being emotional IS feeling! And that's it! Put another way, most of us learn that our emotions are all that we can feel!

Watching Others

When you were very young you were likely to have been taught that feeling is a *noun* and not a *verb*. You were taught that your feelings 'happened to you'. That other people and circumstances are responsible for what you feel. You were taught that when you are excited it is happiness. But it's not. Excitement is your emotional creation when stimulated by something outside your self. It's an agitation of your consciousness. True happiness is a feeling of contentment, blissfulness, or a pure joy that arises from within, for no reason! When you feel excited watching someone win or lose a competition on TV for example, it means that you are attached to and identified with them and their efforts. It's as if you are going through what they are going through in your own mind.

Emoting for Others!

As you watch them perform you generate the emotions of sadness (loss) or elation (winning), with much excitement and fear in the form of tension along the way. While you emote and 'feel' excited, elated or sad, what you won't notice is these are emotions over which you have no control, no choice, because you are attached to, and identified with, the person that you are watching. You have surrendered your self to the images on the screen. In such moments you make your self powerless to choose what you will feel.

In fact, while it seems you are watching their performance on the television you are, in reality, watching them on the screen of your mind. That's where you lose your 'self' in the images of them, in their story. That's where you use them to create an ego based on the image of them. From the attachment/ego comes your emotional disturbances. And so it is that we learn to 'emote for others'!

The Absence of Unhappiness

It's also likely you were taught to believe that happiness was the acquisition and accumulation of stuff! But it's not. That's attachment!

But it's a belief that ensures you will create a sense of self, based on external objects and or people, all of which must eventually leave or be taken away. So fear, as insecurity, must arise. That's why insecurity reigns in the consciousness of, well, just about everyone, every day!

You were taught that happiness is relief from pain. But it's not. That's just the absence of unhappiness, after much emotional suffering that you created in response to some physical pain!

These and many similar illusions around happiness are handed down not so much in books, but by and through the examples and the language of our parents, teachers and media generated characters whose beliefs and perceptions we consume as we grow up. They knew not that they were bequeathing a certain lack of self-awareness and an inability to discern the real meaning of the emotions that we create and feel. They knew not, what they themselves had not been taught! They knew not that they were handing on myths and illusions that would become the basis of our delusions and confusions for the rest of our life. And yet, it was meant to be that way... obviously!

PAUSE

Experiment today. Whenever you start to feel any form of the emotions of anger or sadness see if you can consciously choose to feel something different such as peaceful and contented. Then, as you try, notice what you are attached to in your mind? What are you holding on to, and losing your self in, on the screen of your mind, that is blocking your ability to choose your feelings?

Third IN Sight

Why is there so much confusion about emotions?

If you ask ten people their understanding of emotion you would likely receive ten different, probably wildly different, answers. Then ask them the difference between emotions and feelings and it's not long before further confusion sets in. Apart from that hole in the middle of our education called 'self-understanding' the main reason we are so unclear is that ALL emotions have their roots in attachment.

We are taught to build our lives around becoming and being attached to something or someone. We are taught that our sense of security can only be based on what we accumulate and achieve - which are attachments. We are brilliantly programmed to watch others, identify with others, want what others have, aspire to others' lifestyles and others' apparent success. But that's just more attachment to images and ideals. This is why many of us live a life of perpetual anxiety, tension, resentment and insecurity, to name but a few of the resulting emotions. Then we wonder where and how we are going to find inner peace and happiness. Then we start to seek relief from our emotional suffering in substances and in relationships. More attachments! Dependency and the mindset of the 'victim' must follow.

Attachment ensures that the currency of exchange in our relationships will largely be emotional. 'You are mine' just means I am attached to you. 'That is mine' just means I am attached to it. 'That is going to be mine' just means I am attached to it 'in here' (in my mind) before it arrives in manifest form 'out there'. All of those attachments then generate the fear of loss, sadness after loss, and anger when someone else is seen as responsible for the loss. Hence the cycle of emotion which moves from sadness to anger to fear to sadness to anger to fear. It becomes the 'emotional sound track' to our life. We will eventually compare our 'sound track' with others during our cappuccino conversations as if to confirm and take comfort in sharing many common emotional notes. We will collude to arrive at our joint conclusion that this is the way life is meant to be, an emotional rollercoaster! So we settle for a life of emotional suffering without realizing it!

Addictive and Exhausting

It's not long until we look forward to a good cry as it releases any suppressed emotions. We indulge in outrage, perhaps at fictional characters at first. Then it shows up in our relationship with real people in daily life. We justify our worry about what might happen to others, believing it to be a sign of caring, of showing our love, without realizing we are lost in a mental illusion that confuses fear with love. Any excitement means we are indulging in a temporary escape from our emotional confusions, without realizing that excitement itself is an addictive and exhausting emotional state. We cannot see that the excitement we believe is happiness is just the result of a temporary stimulation, which is, in reality, signaling another attachment!

Disentangling all those states, or distortions of our consciousness, into identifiable emotions becomes the 'big work' of awareness and attention. Not to mention the need to learn a new language to describe what's going on in the inner territory of our consciousness. In the age of exponential busy-ness who's got the time and the inclination for that? Besides, isn't that what we pay a therapist to do for us?

The only way to banish any confusion you may have around the emotions that you create and feel is to a) become more aware of what you are feeling b) whenever you become emotional name the emotion that you are feeling and c) quietly explore what is causing the emotion. This builds your language as well as your self-understanding as you start to notice why you are creating each and every emotion.

One way to do this is to find a friend for some regular cappuccino conversations. Have many full-on conversations focused around: what are emotions; where do they come from; why do they arise; who is responsible for our emotional states; how do we restore our ability to choose what we feel; why would we want to? It's through such conversations that you expand your awareness and build both your understanding and your ability to articulate what and how you feel. However there are three 'be carefuls'!

The first 'be careful'

A big mistake we tend to make is to attribute our emotional creations to someone else. So it's easy to start talking about what others are doing/have done and shouldn't be doing. After a while you'll notice that's just a subtle ploy to avoid facing and talking about your self and the emotions that you are creating and feeling.

The second 'be careful'

As you articulate what and how you feel or felt don't get lost in a story, which is usually code for 'I was the victim in this situation and I need to get your sympathy'. At the mental and emotional level you are never a victim. That's tough to realize but test it your self. Say exactly that to someone and then explain to them why that is so. You'll be surprised at the deeper truth you are able find within and how much conviction you feel when you share it with another.

The third 'be careful'

It seems obvious, but as you tell any 'story of emotion' watch you don't start to re-create the emotions in the story and let them take over again. You will at first. Experiment with being a dispassionate third party in your own story, as you share your own experience, and gradually your understanding of emotions will become clearer, as will their cause.

PAUSE

Take a piece of paper. Write down your memory of a situation in which you reacted emotionally, where you became upset. Put six headings in a column down the left side as follows: perception – thoughts – emotions – ego - behavior - outcome. These are the ingredients, the six main levels, within your REACTION. Then re-run the scenario in slow motion in your mind and write down what occurred within you at each level. Then, on the right side, go through the same event as if you could choose to RESPOND differently. Replace the emotions within your reaction with chosen feelings in a more considered response. This time you are not attached to anything, so there is no ego, therefore no emotion, but you do choose to feel something towards the other person/s or the event. Choose feelings that are not forms of stress or suffering.

If you would like The Worksheet for this reflection send me an email at mike@relax7.com.

Fourth  IN Sight

Why is emotion often ignored in a spiritual context?

You could say all contexts in life, which means all our relationships in life, are spiritual, simply because we are all spiritual beings creating our life experiences. You could say all experiences are spiritual experiences because it's spirit, which is the self, that is experiencing. However, the 'quality' of most experiences tends not to be highly spiritual - simply because they are shaped and distorted by some form of attachment.

They are not consistently peaceful experiences because resentments and judgments, caused by our attachment/ego, disturb our inner peace. They are not consistently loving experiences as we distort our spiritual feelings into the emotions of fear and anger. They are not consistently joyful and authentically happy experiences because we create moments of sadness and sorrow so frequently. All caused by our habit of attachment and the creation of our many faces of ego!

Community Spirit in a Spiritual Community

A 'spiritual context' could be defined as a group of people who are in a conscious process of restoring their true sense of self as spiritual and not physical beings. 'Spirituality' could be loosely defined as *the intentions, thoughts, feelings and behaviors that arise naturally from our true nature as a spiritual being.* That 'nature' is naturally loving (not Hollywood love!), naturally joyful and naturally peaceful. We have all learned to sabotage our own true nature and make our self suffer.

Clean and Clear

We can only be our true self, which means peaceful, loving and joyful, when the energy of our consciousness, of our self, is radiating outwards freely, cleanly and clearly. And that is only possible when there are no attachments to distort your energy on the way out! That means your heart, which is essentially your consciousness, which is you, has to be clean and clear of attachment if you are to know and feel love. That means clean and clear of any desire, which is just another form of attachment. Only when you are free of all attachment can you stop creating fear and anger. As soon as you create an attachment, the vibration of your energy changes from love into fear. Fear is love distorted by attachment – same energy, different vibration, different 'feeling'!

Pressing Each Others Buttons

It's often easier to avoid exploring and understanding the emotions that we create and feel than it is to try to work out why we are emoting. Especially when there is so much confusion around the cause and the meaning of emotion. Many 'spiritual movements' often consign any emotional understanding to the territory of therapy, and therefore deem emotion to be 'unspiritual'. It is sometimes seen to be a 'messy' aspect of spiritual development, throwing up all sorts of feelings, all kinds of emotionally fuelled reactions, the exact nature of which, are hard to agree on, never mind understand.

Most of us are also a little scared of the emotional reactions of others so we prefer not to confront another at that level in case they lapse into an emotional state. That's also when we fear our own emotions in reaction to theirs! Or we fear having to spend time and energy either defending our self from their emotions or helping them recover from their emotional disturbances. While we may try to avoid pressing the wrong buttons in others we also tend to hide our own buttons in the presence of others! These are all probably sensible things to do when we don't really understand what emotion is and why both our own and others emotions 'flare' in the first place. But it can and does lead to suppression, and ultimately repression, as we store up the emotional suffering. It is then likely to explode on some fateful day in the future or just continuously 'leak out' through our sensitive and perhaps unstable personality.

Bypassing Your Emotions

Some spiritual communities and philosophies appear to completely bypass emotions and feelings, not out of avoidance, but out of an understanding that you need to 'transcend' them. Or that you just need to re-learn how to 'have good feelings' towards everyone and everything! That can be (but is not always) code for: just get straight back to your highest state of being, your true spiritual state, your original, eternal and pure state of consciousness. They teach that if you do, then all the 'emotional stuff' below, all the attachment and ego stuff below, will resolve itself. It will disappear naturally because you have accessed and restored the higher and purer reality of your consciousness. They would advise that if you do that then those troublesome emotional disturbances will cease to have power over you and will eventually disappear.

In some ways this seems to be the best approach, for some! Otherwise it's easy to get stuck trying to fathom our emotions, trying to get a grip of our feelings, wrestling with our attachments and trying to destroy the ego, which is, in the end, an illusory sense of self. Who wants to spend time and energy grappling with an illusion? Besides, all this 'trying', all this effortful way to 'deal' with these inner movements of our consciousness is often both tiring and frustrating. It makes no sense to turn our spiritual journey, our re-awakening to who we really are, into some inner struggle for supremacy over an illusion; over what is not real. Why not just be real? Well that's one approach and, for some, it seems to work. But for others it just doesn't work at all.

Spiritual Ankles

Perhaps that's because if you try to be in that high, pure and attachment-free state of consciousness, without clearing some of the weeds from the pathway there, so to speak, then it's likely that those emotions and those attachments will be suppressed, or temporarily side-stepped. They await a trigger, a signal, to jump back up and create their emotional havoc. They are waiting to 'interfere' with any attempt to restore and maintain your highest consciousness as they reach up, like a monster from the deep, grip you by the spiritual ankles and pull you back down into the darkest depths of illusion and emotional suffering. And that seems to be what happens to many on their way back to being their authentic self. One minute they are increasing the purity and power of their consciousness, as they seem to be becoming more real, more their true self, therefore more calm and caring. The next moment they are back drowning in emotional currents that they thought had been dissolved back into the ocean of the self itself, long ago!

This is why what is IN the way IS the way. It's not that we need to wrestle and defeat our emotions (sadness, anger, fear); it's not that we need to painfully give up our attachments (the cause of all our sadnessess, angers and fears); it's not that we need to kill the ego in a bloody inner battle to the death (though some seem to try all three in their spiritual life!). But we do need to understand these inner perversions of our consciousness and thereby 'notice' how they frequently arise to get IN the way of our being our true self. Only then can we see them for what they are, illusions that are based on what is not real. Illusions that dissolve in the reality of the pure light of our own radiant being, just as mist and fog evaporate when exposed to the direct light of the sun.

Being a Source of Love

Hence the gradual effectiveness of spiritual practices like meditation and contemplation. Plus the value of deep, spiritual, but gentle conversations with others on the what, why and how we feel what we feel. Including mutual investigations around what it means to wake up and restore our self, our consciousness, our spirit, to its purest level. Conversations that explore questions like: who am I really; what does it really mean to be 'no one'; how do I be authentic?; are priceless conversations alongside any spiritual practices.

As you meditate, study and discuss, you naturally start to restore your ability to discern the often subtle differences between the unreal and the real within your own being. You invoke your original egoless state of consciousness, which was and is free of all attachment and misidentification, and therefore free of all emotion. You realize that emotionlessness does not mean you become a cold, hard and unfeeling person. Quite the opposite. You notice that love has many expressions and happiness has many subtle textures, all of which you could not feel, experience or express when you were so busy with your emotions.

Can you see emotion and know it for what it is, the product of attachment and the sound of the ego's cries for attention and usually approval? Can you then sense the spiritual journey for what it is, the natural releasing of all attachment, the exposing of all those false identities and the consequent death of the ego and its emotional offspring? Do you recognize that when the awakening of the authentic self begins, emotions will gradually cease to interfere? They just won't get the same amount of attention and energy. Once you fully realize and know your self as you are, as a source of love, as a source of peace, as a source of joy in the world, both your attachments and emotions will naturally lose their power to shape you and disturb you. You will simply stop creating them.

Benevolent Intentions

Why? Because the reason you become attached to anything in the first place is because you **learned to believe** that you needed to SEEK and FIND sources of love and peace and joy, which you also **learned to believe** could only be found in the world outside your self. Once you fully realize that whoever and whatever you have become dependent upon can never fulfill you, can never be a source of the love that you seek; once you fully realize that love is what you are and what you are here to do; that's when a) those beliefs lose their power over you and b) 'they' (other people) become 'opportunities' for you to share, to give, of your self. That's when you start to know your self as the very energy that you used to seek from others. You realize love is what you are!

As soon as you restore unconditionality to your 'giving' of your self, then the habit of attachment starts to naturally wane and lose its power over you. With craving and neediness disappearing you become a source *for* others of what you once sought *from* others. In such moments you know you are awakening... again! How? You will 'feel' the power that arises within your own benevolent intentions, within your own motivation to serve others. Where before you disempowered yourself by wanting and expecting *from* others and becoming dependent *on* others, you re-empower your self by giving *to* others. Not because you have to, or you need to, or even want to, but because that's the natural thing to do, arising from the natural free and loving being that you are.

Subconscious Roots

But it's seldom that straightforward, simply because of the subconscious. All those memories of long established patterns of attachment, all the habits of attaching and misidentifying, are recorded and rooted in your subconscious. So the sources of your emotional disturbances tend to be largely outside your day-to-day and moment-to-moment awareness. But if your spiritual effort, the effort of self-awakening, is consistent, then the practice of meditation will also lower the line between conscious and subconscious, revealing what you are still grasping and wanting. Regular contemplation, especially in silence, gradually reveals the layers of illusory selves recorded in your subconscious. You will see how it's your attachment to these illusions that's generating your 'emotional reactions', and therefore your own suffering.

Hence one of the signs that you are making some 'spiritual progress', signs that an awakening is truly occurring, will be a gradual reduction in the frequency, intensity and the eventual disappearance of all emotion.

Reprioritizing Your Time

It's not easy to unravel, identify and clearly see the cause of your emotions unless you do your own inner work of self-awareness and self-understanding. Only then can you be your own authority both about and within your own consciousness, your own self. Unless you become your own authority you are still dependent on others' views and opinions on such matters. Becoming and being that authority does require you to cultivate a level of self-awareness and self-understanding that ultimately cannot be taught. It has to come from within your self. That will depend on how deeply interested and genuinely curious you are. If you are deeply interested it means you will likely need to reprioritize some of your time and attention. Something will have to 'give', as they say. That 'something' usually involves releasing or spending less time with some of your... attachments!

What you read here is not the gospel on ego and emotion. It has no power to change you, free you, or even enlighten you. That happens only when you see, understand and know for your self.

There are signposts here. But ultimately you will create and follow your own path as you evolve your own clarity on the subject of your 'self', for your self! Then you can erect your own signposts. Then you can create your own way to see it and say it. Then you can write your own gospel... so to speak!

An Experiment without Identity

The destination of any authentic spirituality is the realization of your self as pure consciousness, pure awareness. That means no identity based on anything in this material world. Possible? Most would probably say no, and if it was what would be the point of life?

And yet we all have moments, perhaps you can remember your last moments, when you were 'in' this exact state of being. You would not have described it as being without identity. It was just a moment when you forgot everything, when your consciousness was empty of all worries of the future, concerns in the present, dark memories from the past. You were simply in a kind of empty state. Not a state of emptiness, that's a state that follows the belief you have lost something or someone precious.

You just forgot who you mistakenly thought you are, for a moment, and it 'felt' rather good. You felt rather free and at peace, and very relaxed. The world was indeed a beautiful and benevolent place to be in. Some refer to this state of being as 'presence'. You were no longer absent in any of your attachments (memories, imaginations and speculations). You were fully in the present.

Now imagine you could bring that state of being back to the current context of your life. Imagine being fully present in whatever situation you are in. Imagine you could maintain that state as you interact with others and deal with the day-to-day situations as they arose. Imagine bringing that inner lightness and freedom to the meeting, into the kitchen, into a difficult relationship.

Imagine you are also fully aware that you are simply adopting worldly material identities like your name or your position, your nationality or even religion, for the convenience of the scene and interaction. In other words you are 'wearing' a worldly identity but you know it's not you, just as you are aware that the clothes your body wears are not your body. But your body wears them for convenience! So you 'wear' these identities for convenience. But beneath them you are naked. You know they are not you. The real you is the naked and free spirit.

Experiment with this 'awareness' and see how it feels. Imagine it first. Then 'trial it', in real time, in real life situations.

Let it grow. Don't expect anything. Just experiment. And watch. And see. And feel. And play!

PAUSE

Find a quiet space. Sit quietly. Watch quietly what is occurring in your mind. In the quietness of this gentle process of observation notice what wants to disturb your... quietness! It will be a stray thought or a turbulent emotion or perhaps a dark memory. As soon as you see it allow 'it' to pass. It will pass quietly if you allow it. If you resist it in any way it will stop passing, smile at you and start to suck your energy as it makes one big obstinately loud noise within you.

Stop and allow your self to be quiet. Even amidst the noisy jungle of your thoughts and feelings!

Fifth IN Sight

Do emotions have a natural place in the world?

They may have a place, but it's not a 'natural' one! Human emotions are responsible for climate chaos. It sounds like a big leap from emotion to our weather systems, but if you follow the trail the connection becomes clear. It's all to do with entropy. The entropy of the physical energy that makes up the eco and bio systems of the world is directly related to the entropy of the energy of our consciousness.

The second law of thermodynamics, often referred to as the Law of Entropy, is roughly defined as: *in a closed system all energy moves from an ordered state to a chaotic state.* Set fire to a table and the trapped and ordered energy in the wood of the table is released into a more chaotic state as heat and light. That energy then spreads to fill the room. If we wanted to get that energy back to its previously ordered state in the form of wood, we would need to use more energy than was released. We would have to take that energy from somewhere else. Thereby creating entropy elsewhere. Set fire to all the tables and chairs in the room and soon the temperature of the room rises. The plants start to die and the wallpaper starts to curl off the walls!

Hence the conclusion of entropy, according to the scientific community, is something called 'heat death'. Only a source of energy from outside the enclosed system, in this case it's a room, can restore the energy within the system to an ordered state.

The Suns UP!

Now think of the eco/bio systems of our physical world. For thousands of years the entropy of the natural energy forms within the enclosed systems of the physical world has been slow. So slow as to go unnoticed. Why, because every day a source of energy from outside the system injects new energy into the system, which then restores, refreshes and reorders the energy within the system. Otherwise known as the sun!

However, during the last hundred years we have been releasing the trapped energy from it's many natural 'forms' within the eco/bio system faster than the sun can restore and re-order. There is now an exponentially increasing level of chaos of the energies within the closed eco/bio systems of planet earth. One symptom of that chaos is increasing climate instability and extreme weather events, which seems to include a gradual overall rising in temperature.

Physical Forms and the Formless Spirit

There is another clear distinction between the physical energy of matter and the spiritual energy of consciousness. In the physical world physical energy takes many natural forms. When physical energy is in its many natural material forms it means the energy is in a state of order. Form equals order. It is in a balanced, harmonious and unchaotic state. Whereas the energy of consciousness, in it's most natural state, takes no form! In consciousness, formlessness equals order, while form equals disorder!

Spirit (consciousness) does not take the form of a body, it occupies and animates a body. It can guide and influence the form of the body as it grows, but consciousness, what some call the soul or spirit, is not the form of the physical body! The energy of consciousness is in its most natural state when it is formless and radiating freely outwards from its source, which is itself, the self!

When we do that we are giving of our self unconditionally and in an unlimited way. Sometimes it's called love! It feels consistently good because it is our natural state. We are radiating the energy of our consciousness from a state of complete inner 'formless' freedom. We don't have to decide to do it, or think about doing it. It just is being done!

However, as human beings we have learned to attempt to trap the energy of our consciousness in 'form'. Not physical forms, but in the mental forms of ideas, images, memories, concepts and beliefs. In other words whenever we create 'thought forms' and try to 'preserve' those forms, hold on to those forms, we trap our consciousness, which is our self, within those forms. We are then what is known as 'attached'. Then, when whatever we are attached to (an image/idea in here in our mind) is threatened, moved, damaged or lost we create an energetic disturbance in our consciousness called 'emotion'.

Emotion is chaos in consciousness. Emotion is the equivalent of an extreme weather event in the environment of our consciousness. Some emotional events are more extreme than others. Emotional chaos is the 'heating' of consciousness.

Quick summary.

Physical energy, in its most natural and ordered state, takes many forms. These forms make up what we call our physical environment. Spiritual energy, the energy of consciousness, in its most natural state, takes no form. It is (i.e. you are) formless and 'designed' to freely radiate outwards from its source, the self (you again), in all directions at all times. Release the physical energy from the many material forms and the energy moves to an entropic state of chaos. Try to trap the energy of consciousness in the form of any idea, image etc. (attachment) and the energy of consciousness moves into an entropic state known as 'emotional chaos'.

Quick reminder.

Love is not an emotion. You are not emoting when you are genuinely caring, compassionate, kind and giving – just a few of loves many expressions. Authentic happiness is not an emotion. You are not emoting when you are content or joyful – the two main states of human happiness.

Now, here's the key point. Emotion is addictive. Excitement, fear, anger and sadness are primary emotions and they are all addictive. While emotion is an unnatural and chaotic state for the energy of consciousness to be in, it is both addictive and exhausting. We have seen how all emotion arises when the self creates a mental form within consciousness, within the self, and then tries to 'preserve it' by becoming attached to it. So emotional chaos within the energy of consciousness is the result of trying to give the energy of consciousness a permanent form.

As a result the most common emotion is excitement. When you are excited the origin of the excitement appears to be in the world. But it's not, that's an illusion. The origin of excitement is within your consciousness, within your mind. What 'triggers' you to create the emotions of excitement, sadness, anger and fear? It could be a person or an event out there in the material world. They don't 'cause' your emotional disturbance but they are 'triggers'. You pull that trigger and you recreate an 'emotional flaring' in the environment of your own being.

Two Examples: Two football fans of the Red Team are walking down the road on their way to the game. They both have two children so they are talking calmly and sensibly about how beautiful their children are. Then, around the corner comes a group of fans of the Blue Team. This triggers the two Red Team fans to create an image in their minds of the Red Team and the thought form, 'I am

Red Team'. They attach to, and identify with, that thought form. They create a little fear and perhaps a little excitement or even anger, because they see the Blue Team fans as a threat to their identity as Red Team. From a state of calm they disturb themselves with the emotions of fear and excitement. Why? Because they recreate an image of the Red Team in their minds and attach themselves to that image thereby identifying with that image. They use the Blue Team fans as a trigger to create animosity (anger) and tension (fear).

Two women walking down the high street are chatting warmly about their husbands going to get their weekly emotional fix at the game! They pass the handbag shop. One says, "Look aren't those Gucci hand bags just the best?" The other, who already has three Prada handbags at home, brings up the image of Prada in her mind. She sees herself as a 'Prada person', and says defensively, "Nah, Prada is much better". A friendly argument ensues which then escalates into a little exchange of anger in the form of frustration and irritation with each other. They are also giving themselves their emotional fix! Why? Because they are recreating the image (forms) of the brand names in their minds and then attaching themselves to that image.

In both cases they tried to give the energy of their consciousness a form - an image of a team and image of brand. As a result they created the emotions of... well, you get the picture! This is why when you create forms in your consciousness and hold on to those forms you will inevitably generate emotional heat.

Creating Chaos in a Safe Space

Watch all the emotions you create when you go to a movie. Then see if you can see why you 'feel' those emotions. It's always because you create a form in your mind - the mental form of an image or an idea. Then you become attached to that 'mental form' as you try to hold onto it, preserve it. You cry with sadness when someone in the story loses something. You create frustration and even anger when someone does something that you decide you don't like in the story. Why? Because they are not doing or being according to an image that you have created in your mind of how they 'should' do/be. You create fear when someone in the movie is about to lose something, usually their life, or a pain free state! So many movies and they all give you a reason, a stimulus, the raw material, to create the chaos of emotion in your consciousness. They are triggers but not causes.

We create these emotions in the safe space of the movie theatre or our own lounge. It's the unnaturalness, the edginess, of these emotions of excitement or fear or anger that we then believe makes us feel vital and alive. To believe and perceive them to be natural suits us, as it allows us to indulge in our emotional drugs without threat or conscience. One dictionary defines emotion as *agitation of mind*. Excitement is agitation. It's unnatural to be agitated. But before you know it you are craving more agitation, so you are waiting for the next movie, the next episode, the latest, more shocking, more sorrowful, more fearful movie. Then along you go to indulge your addiction in the belief that it's the movie that is making you 'feel' these emotions. But in truth it's you that creates these moments of chaos in your consciousness.

Feeling Good is Not So Good

Even the so-called 'feel good' movies are usually sentimental stories at which you create the sentimental emotions of sadness and sorrow. Sometimes you use the movie to trigger a catharsis of accumulated sadness, after which you feel lighter. Until it builds up again and then it's off to the next movie for another good cry.

Over time we require ever more shocking, graphic, crude and disastrous images in order to give us the raw material with which we can generate the emotions and will satisfy our addiction. Rather like a drug addict who progressively requires a more powerful drug to achieve the same high. Add to that the marketer's dream world where the vehicles of entertainment and people's ability to 'plug in' to other people's lives, increases exponentially in the space of two decades. Technology reigns. It delivers instantly, the stimulations (images and ideas) that we use to generate our emotional fix. It streams directly into our minds 'idea forms' and 'image forms' which we then re-create and attach our self to within our consciousness. Then when something happens to those forms we create the agitation, the fears and the angers, the sorrows and the relief, in other words the 'entropic chaos of emotion' within the system of our consciousness.

People's attention span is reduced to seconds as they keep looking at their phones for the latest email, text and tweet which, when read, is a great excuse to create a little moment of excitement, sadness, anger or fear. Hence the exponential rise in the development and use of technology in the last twenty years. Hence the rapid increase in the production of movies, videos, websites, twittering, facebooking, emailing, texting and all the other ways to deliver examples of thought forms that we then re-create and attach our self to. Technology is a syringe for the soul!

For some people just a two-line text message can mean emotional devastation for the rest of the day. It's exhausting yet addictive. Then, after months of emotional exhaustion it's time for a break, for a holiday, for a rest. But we then take our sophisticated machines, our ipads and ipods, epads and tripods, to the beach and we up the speed of our texting and tweeting and surfing and facebooking.

Developers and Deliverers

To sustain this exponential explosion of emotional stimulation requires we manufacture faster and better technology... every year!

That necessitates the release of more and more physical energy from its natural forms. The developers require more physical energy to design and develop more clever gadgets with which to deliver more sounds, images and ideas to an ever expanding and thirsty audience. The entertainment industry requires more physical energy to increase the sophistication and the output of movies and games. The social media platforms need more physical energy to receive, store and deliver more 'entertainment', more efficiently. We all need more energy to plug in, recharge and interconnect more machines for our daily fix! The airlines require more fuel to take more emotionally exhausted people to more places more frequently to supposedly rest and refresh. It ALL requires that we extract more physical energy faster from the natural world around us. Thereby increasing the rate of entropy, the rate of chaos in the environment.

Global Emotional Warming

The emotional heat within the environment of our consciousness, which is both addictive and exhausting, is a direct result of our attachments; i.e. our attempt to give form to the energy of our consciousness. The increasing number of people who have access to the images and ideas delivered by modern technologies can only be sustained by the use of more and more physical energy. This means that it's the habit of giving form to the energy of our consciousness so that we can generate emotion that is the underlying cause of our releasing more and more trapped energy from its natural physical forms in the world.

Global 'emotional warming' is responsible for global environmental chaos. The ego and the resulting emotions within human consciousness, are slowly killing the planet.

Like those solar flares we sometimes see in pictures of the sun, our consciousness flares outwards or inwards when we are emotional. We tend to let our self be carried along on the flare. So when we create anger or sadness we go *with* the emotion, we go *into* the emotion, into the flaring. Even saying, "I am very angry", or "I am so depressed" or "I am so excited". This is why staying cool isn't about looking cool. It's about detaching from the forms we are trying to create and preserve in our consciousness. Being cool means learning to come out of the emotion and just watching the flaring, knowing it will, like a bushfire, eventually recede and die. Staying cool is staying in your centered state, where you are not attached to any mental form.

Open to the Source

The physical energy of the material world is meant to take many forms, but the energy of consciousness is meant to open and unformed. The external source of energy that maintains the formed and ordered energies of the physical world is the sun. Each day it gives of itself as light and heat and almost every living creature and plant in the world absorbs that light and is sustained and strengthened. Entropy is kept at bay, until we interfere and release the energy faster than the sun can replace it.

It is also an external source of energy that restores the openness and unformed state of our consciousness. This source of spiritual energy is sometimes referred to as 'The Source'. Just as the flower draws light and heat from the sun and creates a form that is beautiful, fragrant and colorful, so the 'self' draws the warmth of pure love and the light of enlightenment from 'The Source'. It does so to create a state of being that is free, spiritually beautiful with a fragrance of character in which others may perceive that beauty. When the flower connects to the sun it knows it is a flower and does not try to be a bush or a tree. When the soul, the self, connects to the energy of the source it ceases trying to create, adopt and identify with any form. It is restored to its most natural state of formlessness. It knows itself only as the 'I' that says 'I am'. Which is no one! And that is enough.

Sixth IN Sight

How do we manage and dissolve emotions after they arise?

What I am NOT saying here is that emotion is wrong or bad. It's probably easy to perceive and interpret what I am saying in this way. Our dualistic conditioning (it's either good or bad, right or wrong etc.) leads us to 'interpret' in such black and white ways. As we have seen, 'emotion' is always the result of attachment to, and identification with, something that is not 'me'. It 'happens' in our own mind. So emotion is just a 'consequence' of a mistaken identity. Emotions are therefore also just mistakes. They will continue to be 'triggered', but not caused, by people and events, by circumstances and the demands of the world around us. Until we have fully awoken to who we are, the past recordings, the oldest memories, the subconscious habits, our deeply embedded attachments, our mistaken identities, will all throw up emotional storms within the energy of our consciousness. Emotion is after all Energy in **MOTION**. So how do we deal with the 'unexpected arrival' of our emotions, i.e. the emotions that 'seem' to occur for absolutely no reason?

Answer: with a great deal of difficulty! Unless there are specific practices that you have integrated into your life, emotion will tend to run your life. As we explored in the previous chapter, most cultures in the world today are fueled by and run on emotion. They are the addiction that we all share. The main practices that will help you manage and ultimately free you from the habit of 'emoting' are the same as those necessary to 'see through' the illusions created by the ego, namely the practices of meditation and contemplation. The first step of meditation is often referred to as 'detached observation'. This is the practice of detaching from what is happening in your mind. It's as if you come 'out of your mind' and return to your inner seat within your consciousness so that you can watch what arises in your mind.

It can be likened to watching the movie and not losing your awareness that you are in your seat in the cinema and that the movie is quite a separate fictional event happening 'up there' on the screen. As long as you maintain that awareness you won't get 'sucked in' to the movie, which means you won't get lost in the story that you create, based on the movie, in your own mind. The more you practice just watching what is occurring on your mind the more you will get a sense of your self as 'the observer' and the more you will cease attaching to, and identifying your self with, any idea, image, character, that you create in your mind. Then your mind becomes your servant where before it felt like you were its slave!

When you cease to lose your self *in* and identify *with* what's on your mind only then do you start to take back your power as you restore mastery of your consciousness. Sometimes this is referred to as self-mastery. But it's not so much mastery of the self but mastery of all that you can do with and within your consciousness, within you!

So the next time you make a suggestion or come up with a crazy idea and someone says to you, "Are you out of your mind"? Just say 'yes thanks'!

Meditation in Five Steps

As we saw earlier, those habits of attachment/misidentification go deep into our subconscious. When triggered we feel waves of emotion rise from those depths! Sometimes we call them moods. When they come it's like a signal to move into our meditative practice and contemplative process, for a few moments at least.

Step One - be fully aware of the emotions that you are feeling. If possible name the emotion/s that is/are arising.

Step Two - fully acknowledge the presence of the emotion/s and that you are fully responsible for creating the emotion/s that you feel. That may require correcting the false belief that 'it's not me, it's them that is making me feel like this' and acknowledging that 'it's me, not them'. Be patient. Keep reminding your self that it's your creation but not you. But don't beat your self up over it! It's just the result of a mistaken sense of self. You are 'in the process' of correcting your mistake/s.

Step Three - But don't resist your creation, which means don't suppress or repress the emotion. Don't express it either, if you can. Accept it. Talk to it! The moment you do you will notice your mood lifting and gradually you will be less susceptible to emotional triggers!

Step Four - Start to ascend. This means adopt the position of the detached observer as if you are clearly aware that there is you and there is the emotion, quite separate. You are not really separate but the effort helps you pull out of the flaring of emotion, thus denying it life. Experiment with just observing the emotion, without being moved by it, as quickly as possible after it arrives.

Step Five - is the process of attuning to the center of you. That's where you always find your peace, which is your power. The process of 'tuning in' to the center of your being is the practice of meditation. You 'tune out' all other extraneous energies and noises from your attention so that there is just you. It sounds easy in theory but it takes practice simply because we have become addicted to distraction. We live in the age of distraction! Withdrawing our attention from the world around us, even for a few moments, is challenging for many. Being able to withdraw your attention from your emotional flares is an inner practice that eventually restores your ability to choose your feelings.

Experiment with these five steps until you don't need them. Ultimately meditation is not driven by method but by intention. Eventually it becomes a natural way to create your state of being free of any and all emotion.

The art and practice of meditation is the self, acknowledging to itself, that it's time to realize for my self who I am and what I am and how I work, within me! Meditation is the cultivation of self-awareness. It eventually requires no teacher, no special time, no particular approach. There is no one right way to meditate, no correct method to become self-aware. It is not just something to add to your 'to do' list, and it is not an achievement, it is not a goal. It is an ongoing process of personal enlightenment/awakening as you see and realize with increasing clarity what is true and what is false, what is real and what is unreal, within... your self!

PAUSE
For the simplest meditation
Sit somewhere quiet
Rest your gaze on a point somewhere in front of you
Relax your body and your eyes
Watch your breath for a moment
Bring your awareness to your self
Be aware of your self, being aware of your self
If anything external distracts you, come back and start again
If any thoughts or feelings arise to distract you, let them pass
Create one thought, 'I am peace and I am still'
Feel peaceful and be still
Silent and still... silent and........... still!

Seventh IN Sight

How do we deal with emotions that arise from past traumas?

From a spiritual point of view we are, in one sense, all traumatized! And yet we're not! So lets get deep!

The moment we invested our sense of identity in something that we are not then the self-created suffering that characterizes trauma at a spiritual level is inevitable. To create an ego is to self inflict a trauma! It's a shock to the true nature of the soul, which starts out as the pure, unpolluted, unattached, free and radiant energy of consciousness. We all 'learn' to create a false sense of identity. The emotional suffering that must follow, then grows, over time, perhaps over many lifetimes, in its intensity. As it grows, some of that suffering, and for some people a lot of that suffering, is habitually suppressed; i.e. 'pressed' down into the subconscious.

It's our true nature to freely radiate the light of our consciousness outwards in a vibration we call love. When we do we are 'being our natural self'. Then, when we fall asleep spiritually and create a false identity for our self, it distorts the energy of the self from love into fear. To fear is to suffer. This is also 'traumatic' for the soul/self. Soon after, we will start to create and 'feel' the 'vibrations' of sadness and anger. We will eventually come to name these vibrations/feelings the 'emotions' of sadness and anger. These are also traumatic moments for the soul, for the self, simply because they are violations of (violence against) our true nature. Unfortunately we will learn to tolerate these emotions. Eventually we will learn to mistakenly believe they are natural and we will even come to identify with them and become addicted to them.

All such moments then become memories or 'recorded information' within our consciousness, in what we call the subconscious. Over time, these recordings become a burden within our consciousness. They become what are sometimes referred to as 'our karma', which is the record of all our physical, mental and emotional creations. Like one big heavy weight slows down a truck, and then subsequent weights slow it down even more, so our consciousness slows. We carry the accumulated weight of the memory of many moments of many traumas caused by our own ego and the resulting emotional disturbances.

System Crash

Each time we repeat the thoughts, feelings and actions of those recordings, our 'karmas' (recorded actions) become deeper and more heavily laden with disturbing emotional memories. A computer will slow down, hang or crash when its memory becomes full of too many programs and too much information. So too, our consciousness will start to exhibit the signs and symptoms of being overloaded with too many 'traumatic recordings' as the habits of creating attachment, ego and emotion are enacted more frequently.

Habits within consciousness are the equivalent to programs in a computer. We all develop habits of believing, perceiving, thinking, emoting and acting. And if these habits are not aligned to the trueness of our being, which of course they aren't if they are based on attachment and ego, they will gradually take up more space, more memory, within our consciousness. The more our memory expands, the more of our energy it needs to maintain itself, the more power it then has to influence our thoughts, decisions and feelings. So we create a vicious cycle, which only increases our attachments and our ego, which then increases the frequency and intensity of our emotional disturbances, which then creates more heaviness, more unhappiness. And here we all are today, living in a world that's generally filled with a great deal of unhappiness!

Emotional Self-Diagnosis

Some of the signs and symptoms of our consciousness being blocked or distorted, laden and slowed, by such memories of our karmas, include: an inability to think clearly; stress or confusion when faced with making choices; the inability to feel happy within one self and loving towards others at will; an inability to remain calm in everyday situations; wayward, reckless and anti-social behavior; obsessive behavior; difficulty in concentrating; it becomes harder to clearly discern and make decisions based on what is accurate and inaccurate; there is a habitual set of behaviors that seek to sabotage a relationship; there are emotional and physical reactions that seem to have no logical cause; there is physical disease as the now deviant energy of consciousness reaches down and distorts the cellular energy of our body.

It can seem as if life is one long laborious struggle under the constant strain of a moodiness that we don't realize is pulling us down. We may even 'crash' within our consciousness when we just can't cope any more and we go into a form of 'overload' or 'shut down' and we 'shut out' the rest of the world. All these 'records of habit', these 'traumatic memories', are essentially what is IN the way of our awakening. They are IN the way of our energy flowing freely, naturally and lightly from the heart of our being out into the world of our relationships. However, as we shall see, the good news is they all have the same single root cause. All we need to do is pull out that one root and we will be well again, free again, light again, our self again! That root is the 'habit' of attaching to, and therefore identifying with, what we are not! Yes, our old friend, the ego!

Therapeutic Solutions

When this 'karmic suffering' increases in intensity most of us have no real idea why we feel heavy, moody and extremely unhappy for no apparent reason. With no obvious cause, people eventually seek help to understand and resolve their mental and emotional suffering. They go searching to find out why they are so stressed or depressed, so frequently angry or continuously insecure, so reactive and perhaps destructive, in their relationships with others.

This is the context in which therapeutic practice arises. There are many therapies that can help the soul/self release the burdens and traumas that it has created, recorded and carried, perhaps for a long time. Perhaps many lifetimes! They range from Past Life Regression Therapy, to Rebirthing Therapy to Inner Child Therapy and many more. They all have a place and their effectiveness will normally depend on a combination of the therapist's skillfulness and the patient's openness.

All such therapies tend to have one aim in common. To unlock our consciousness from a memory, or a sequence of memories, of 'past' traumatic experience/s that keep blocking and/or distorting our thoughts, decisions and behaviors with emotion in the 'present'.

The purpose here is not to review or assess such therapies but to consider what is happening from a purely spiritual point of view. And perhaps to ask the question, does spirituality also come in the same category. Is it also a 'therapy'? Here is one possible answer for your consideration. See if it feels right to you!

Is Spirituality just Another Therapy?

It's all about memory! It's in memory that all those apparent traumas are recorded. It's when those memories are stimulated that the emotional suffering that lives within the memory of the original trauma is triggered and spills back into our present state consciousness. The emotion/s then has the power to shape and influence, sometimes it feels like control, our thoughts, decisions, attitudes and behaviors. We react instead of respond. We find our self 'feeling' what we don't want to feel (emotion). We say things we don't want to say and behave in ways we either regret, or in ways that we know are not an expression of our full potential, or indeed our true self. But we cannot seem to help it.

So how many such memories of trauma, and the related emotions are there? All recorded and embedded in our consciousness. Who knows? Hundreds? Thousands? Do we need to know? Probably not! So now, are you sitting comfortably, as they say? Here is why you may not need therapy!

Being Your Self
When you are being your self, your true self, prior to the creation of any false identities, there is no attachment or misidentification. That's when nothing can touch you. You are invulnerable. You are not thinking that, or even aware of that, you just are... invulnerable. Like a child is invulnerable to a verbal insult before it learns to create a self-image and the language that comes with it. This invulnerability is as much a state of innocence as anything else. So nothing can be said or done that can 'trigger' you to perceive your self to have been harmed. Therefore you never create any form of emotional suffering. You are in a body in the material world, but you have not yet started using anything in the world to build an identity! You are not holding onto anything of the world in your mind. You are not investing your sense of self in anything from the world. You are unattached and free in your being. Able to give the energy of you in its highest vibration, which is love. You have no idea what unhappiness is! You have arrived to fulfill the purpose of life, which

is to live and express (press out) your self through the form that you occupy!

That describes, to some extent, our true and original state of being, from a purely spiritual point of view. It's that same 'starting point' for us all.

Consciousness is Infected
One day you catch a virus called 'attachment'. You learn to create an image in your mind of the body you occupy. You become attached to that image. You start to base your sense of identity on that image of your body. You start to do the same with many 'things' related to your body. Your sense of 'who I am' crystalizes around material things. Then, one day, someone shoots your body with a gun so you believe they have shot 'you'. You are traumatized. Or someone blows up your house in which you have invested your sense of self, your identity. You feel as if 'you' have been destroyed. You even say, "I am devastated". You are traumatized. Today many people say the 'I was devastated' line for a lot less then the loss of a house! Being traumatized also seems to be addictive!

Or... let's say you have developed the belief that you are bright, clever and beautiful, based on your intellectual achievements and your physical appearance. Then, for the first time, someone says you are stupid, dull and ugly. It feels like a knife in the back, and in the leg, and in the stomach, all at the same time! Why? Because you are attached to and identified with the idea/image of being clever, bright and beautiful. So you believe you have been insulted, you are traumatized, by such... cruel words! But what you don't notice is that the feeling of insult, the trauma, is not created by the other, or by their words, or by the event. It is created by you simply because you have forgotten who/what you 'really' are. Simply because your sense of self is based on an idea and an image of being clever, bright and beautiful, which is not you, can never be you, because you are not an idea or an image! So when the insult arrives in your consciousness it's not 'you' that was hurt it was the ego that was hurt. It's always only the ego that is hurt!

This is why the ego is the cause of all suffering, therefore the cause of all trauma. It is the cause of all those traumatic memories, conscious and subconscious, of ALL the traumatic moments on our life journey, perhaps on the journey of many lifetimes. In reality the ego is not the self. That means it's not the 'I' that says 'I am', that is hurt and traumatized, it's the ego. It's our creation that is hurt. But it feels like it's me, it feels like the self has been offended. We take it so personally, because our sense of self is lost in, wrapped up in, our own mental creation.

The inner reality is that there are probably hundreds of such moments of suffering, all recorded, all lurking in our subconscious. All poised for the slightest trigger to spill their emotional contents back into our present state of consciousness. Can we, do we, need to revisit every such memory in order to heal our self, to release our self, from the recorded memories of all our past traumas? From a spiritual point of view the answer seems to be no.

Restoring the Egoless State

One spiritual understanding reminds us that the deepest memory we all carry is when we were egoless. When we were in that invulnerable and unhurtable state. When we were in a state of consciousness which could not be offended or violated and therefore could not 'self traumatize'! It's that original pure state of consciousness that is prior to the virus of attachment, prior to the creation of ego. When we did not identify with anything. When nothing blocked the radiant light of our being on its way from the heart of our being out into the world. When we were just being our true and natural self. We were egoless.

Dissolve and Disappear

This 'spiritual understanding' reminds us that we only need to restore this ever abiding, inner state of being, and be consciously aware of it. Then all other memories and their emotional traumas will cease to have any power over us. It can be likened to the sun rising in the morning and, as it does, it gradually chases away the darkness of the night. The sun doesn't eliminate one shadow at a time. It doesn't go looking for areas of darkness or shadows to 'work on'. It doesn't make any effort to get 'up there' into the sky! It just rises and shines, rises and shines, naturally!

Eventually it rises high enough that the brightness of its light automatically eliminates all shadows in all directions. By raising our consciousness, up and back to its true state, free of attachment, free from ego, that's when those 'shadows', which are those memories of past traumas within our consciousness that: a) generate our emotional reactions b) create our mental confusion and c) obscure the clarity of our intellect, start to disappear... naturally. It's as if they are chased away by the pure light of a pure consciousness in its real, true, authentic and original state. Some call this true spiritual healing.

So that means, in theory at least, all we have to do is touch our original and pure state of consciousness, which is already present within us. Like the sun 'disappears' the shadows, our true state of being will dissolve all those memories of suffering, all the traumas recorded within our consciousness that contain the emotions that we ourselves, in our egotistical state, created in our reactions to those past events.

Hence the efficacy of meditation and yoga. Meditation is a way to reach back in to restore our awareness of our original, non-attached and pure state. From that moment the state of our consciousness is 'enlightened' and we intuitively see that all our suffering was self-created because of one mistake, the ego. It wasn't mum or dad, it wasn't our teacher, it wasn't the accident, it wasn't being rejected or being told we were useless or ugly, that traumatized us. It was our attachment to, and subsequent identification with, what we are not, that was the real root cause of our trauma. It was our own ignorance of our self that 'caused' the trauma.

Enter the Victim Mindset

However, when we mistakenly start to attribute our traumas to other people, or to events, we also create the mindset, the belief, that 'I was a victim'. 'I am a victim' then becomes another false identity and we unknowingly start looking for ways to affirm that identity. Hence the frequency with which some people look for reasons to be offended or violated! This one misidentification alone ('I am a victim') will cause us to create numerous debilitating emotional and mental symptoms. Some will spend their entire life stuck in the illusion, the self-image, of 'I am a victim'.

Like many little vampire bats hanging around in a cave, all these recorded traumas have been hanging around and living within our consciousness. Mostly hanging in our subconscious. As they do they suck the life energy of our consciousness away from being who we are, away from being at peace, away from being a source of love and away from being a contented being! But just as vampires cannot stand being in the sun, indeed they are 'apparently' burnt to ash in the sun (vampire mythology!), so all our past traumas and their emotional remnants, when exposed to the pure light of our enlightened consciousness, are burnt to a cinder and are no more. They are made toast! Which is why any authentic spiritual awakening, which means self-realization, probably makes therapy redundant. But it also means that only we, our self, can raise our consciousness, burn up and disappear the records of our own traumas and their emotional content, and thereby be healed within the spirit that we are.

Cleaning our Consciousness

Which is why many step onto a spiritual path and step off again not long after. It's a deep inner process that does require us to reprioritize just about everything in our life as we shift the focus of our attention and energy in significant ways. Unless and until we do this, our own inner work of raising and purifying our consciousness, it's likely we will revert to seeking the help and support of someone else to do it with us, or under the illusion that they can do it for us. That 'someone' is often a therapist with a particular way or process of exposing and healing some of our recorded traumas. But it seems few, if any, therapies can heal them all, can 'burn up' them all!

It seems to be neither bad nor wrong to seek therapeutic assistance while doing our inner spiritual work of 'waking up' and restoring our true self-awareness. For many it may be totally appropriate until they free themselves from a particularly challenging blockage (karmic recording) that has a particularly powerful trauma at it's root. And for others, who don't want to commit themselves so fully to a 'spiritual way', both approaches may run in parallel until there comes a moment to choose which fork in the road to travel down. Perhaps we just need to be careful that the therapy, and indeed the therapist, doesn't become just another attachment or dependency that we will inevitably have to release at some later stage. Even then however, that may be the best way forward for some, for some of the time! There is just no black and white, no absolute right or wrong way in the process of self-awakening and the healing of the spiritual being that we are

Emotional Contagion

Why emotions are now the primary
'currency of exchange' in the world

Crafty Emotion!

We have been invaded and overrun by an alien force. We are at the mercy of an invisible energy that demands we pay it homage and allow it to enter every area of our daily life. It makes us lazy, indulgent and most of all dependent. It sucks the life out of us as it sabotages the wellness of our being in a hundred different ways.

It has become our master and commander, emerging onto 'the bridge' of our consciousness in order to dictate the direction of our life. It is the primary currency with a variable rate of exchange according to its own whims. It is a parasite that eats into our heart and then leeches out through our behavior. It doesn't seem to know the real meaning of life... or death!

It is emotion.

It is so clever it has led us to believe we know it well, yet we have no idea how it is caused. Strategic emotion. It has led us to embrace and welcome it into our lives by defining itself as a level of human intelligence. Clever emotion. It has convinced us that life would not be worth living without it. Crafty emotion.

It has positioned itself as a priceless resource in all the places where humans generate their wealth. Devious emotion. It has even sold itself as the essential ingredient in the creative purpose of human existence. Hypnotic emotion.

But we are on its case! We are starting to unravel its spell. We are beginning to demystify and reveal its agenda. We are beginning to strip away its illusions and see it for what it really is. Well some are! Others, probably most, are still dancing to its spell. Still using its illusory power to try to manipulate and control, enforce and cajole.

It has increasingly crept into our language over the last twenty years. We have even created many 'terms of endearment' in our acceptance of its presence. For example:

Emotionally Secure

Here is a term used by those who would like us to find security in our relationships through our emotional exchanges with others. Yet emotion, by definition, is an agitated state of consciousness and therefore a state of internal insecurity. Emotion itself is the primary creation and main characteristic of those who are insecure. 'Emotional security' is an oxymoron.

Emotional Health and Wellbeing

"Come to our spa, attend our retreat, if you do our course you will see how you can restore your emotional wellbeing". So runs many a blurb or PR for a place or process that will help you achieve emotional wellbeing. Yet the presence of emotion is a symptom of unwellness. Health is to do with our physical body and wellness is to do with our consciousness. Emotion originates within our consciousness and it is a sign that we are not well in our being. The absence of emotion is necessary to be at peace. The absence of emotion is essential to stay calm, be open, be loving, be content and to give our energy as enthusiasm to others.

Why is it so hard for us to see that what we call 'love' and 'joy' are states of being and not just 'other emotions'? Because no one would go to see the movie, the circus or the match, no one would buy a book about a love story, which is usually a 'sad' story, if there were no emotional dramas. Drama is by definition, about people's emotions. Take out emotion and no one is 'stimulated', take away stimulations and everyone gets bored. You cannot make money by boring people so love is confused with lust, with sadness, with hurt, with pain, with just about every emotion, in order to take advantage of everyone's emotional addiction.

Yes Emotional Healing is a subtitle of this book. That's because emotion is a wound on the soul. It leaves a scar within our consciousness that if touched, just as if a physical scar is touched, will erupt in a moment of pain. Test this for your self. If you create anger towards someone it leaves an impression in 'you'. Then the next time you see them it's as if their image enters your consciousness, it touches the memory of the anger, and guess what, you suffer a moment of anger towards them... again.

Emotional Intelligence

Ah yes, the intelligence that is associated with emotion in these two words that have crept into almost every area of the training, tutoring, self-development and personal growth industries during the last twenty years. Emotional intelligence infers that when you are emotional you are more intelligent! But when we take a moment to reflect we may notice that any time we are emotional we are not capable of being very intelligent! That's because emotion is an 'agitation within consciousness'. And when we are agitated we cannot think very clearly. But more importantly we stop being able to hear the wisdom of our heart, sometimes referred to as our intuition. That's the inner resource of a deeper 'knowingness' that we need to draw on if we are to make intelligent decisions, create intelligent responses and interact with intelligent behavior. All are impossible during any emotional moments. Emotional intelligence is yet another oxymoron.

Emotional Control

It's not possible to control emotion. When emotion arises it is in control of you! All we can do is learn to notice it and not be ruled by it. All we can do is lessen its life span by adopting practices like meditation in which we learn to step back from our emotions as and when they flare. Eventually it is possible to stop creating emotion in the first place. And when that happens then we remain calm and fully attentive, loving and fully available, compassionate and contented, joyous and fully present.

Emotional Exploitation

There is of course an industry 'out there' whose job it is to keep you in an attached, ego-driven and therefore emotional state. It is the marketer and advertisers' job to exploit your habit of believing happiness comes from purchasing and possessing material stuff. It's their job to sustain your aspiration to be like someone else, usually someone famous. They want you to keep building your sense of identity based on the products and the people that they project at you! And so they use images and words that are designed to exploit your weakness for attachment, and the emotional stimulation that comes with it, just like a weakness for sweet things. In one particular advert for a certain car company the strap line brilliantly sums up our relationships with emotion. At the end of the advert, which is filled with the appeal of a sleek and shiny new car, there is an invitation to become attached to the latest model. Then under the manufacturers name there is a new word – AutoEmocion - whispered in a seductive tone. You can only laugh!

Emotional Contagion

Have you ever watched a TV show in which the studio audience screams with apparent excitement at the slightest signal. Prior to the show the audience is briefed and hyped into a highly emotional state and encouraged to give vent to those emotions during the show. Then, as we watch, we wonder why on earth they are so excited about someone jumping into a pool of water, or baking a cake, or just smiling after two lines of dialogue! This is emotional contagion and it's spreading fast and far across the airwaves of the world. Before long it becomes a risk not to join in. The risk of being an outsider, of being someone who doesn't get it! Little do we realize emotion is a contagious mental dis – ease that spreads faster than the flu virus can create its disease in our bodies.

Emotional Abuse

Much has been explored, analyzed and written about what appears to be the growing phenomena known as self-harm. It isn't really 'self harm', it's body harm! Real self-harm is, yes you guessed, emotion! It does not cause pain, it is 'suffering'. But it is a suffering that can seem pleasant, even sweet. It is self-inflicted because no one else is responsible for whatever we create within our own being. The harm it does is to weaken our ability to stay calm and be loving and know true joy – the very purpose of life, some would say.

Emotional Attachment

Which brings us to the frequently used phrase 'emotional attachment'. We often refer to someone being emotionally attached, such as, 'he is emotionally attached to his team' or 'she is emotionally attached to her old car'. However this makes it sound like the emotion comes first and the attachment follows. In reality it's the other way round. The attachment happens first and the emotion follows. It's just that the attachment is a subtle event in our minds and we are not taught how to 'notice it'. So the first thing that tends to be seen by others is the emotional disturbance itself.

PAUSE

A personal research project! Call it the **Hunt for True Meaning!** *Make it your mission to hunt down the true meaning of emotion and feeling, love and happiness, passion and enthusiasm, compassion and care, fear and anger, sorrow and stress, sadness and suffering. Then, once you have compiled your dossier set out to find the interconnection and interrelationship between them all.*

Untangling Emotion, Feeling and State

It is not easy to untangle these three concepts as they all describe something in the invisible universe of consciousness. One of the reasons why our general understanding of them is a little limited, if not skewed, is we don't generally differentiate between consciousness (i.e. the soul/self/spirit) and the brain. We tend to believe that it's all brain, that we are just a brain. That's usually followed by the belief that 'it's my brain chemistry that's in charge, not me, so I can't really do anything about it'. This is lazy believing that leads to lazy thinking and general laziness all round!

However as soon as you become open to the suggestion that the brain is just a material object, a chemical computer, and that YOU are both the programmer and the operator, then you almost instantly start to realize that YOU are in charge and not the chemistry! You can prove to your self that there is you AND your brain by consciously choosing to change a habit, by letting go of an old belief and replacing it with a new truth, by sitting and consciously creating a certain feeling. Those and many other little experiments will naturally lead you to the conclusion that, "I could be fully in charge of everything that goes on within my consciousness, within me". Then you will ask your self why is that not the case all the time? You will start to notice the beliefs, inherited and assimilate in younger years, that are already 'in there' and how you are consciously and subconsciously 'attached' to them. Beliefs are not chemicals they are ideas and concepts from which you have made into forms as you 'formed' your belief system. Then you start to see the effect that your attachment to this 'belief programming' is causing; i.e. much emotional suffering and confusion, or to put it a little more plainly... all your stress and unhappiness!

Only then might you become interested enough to start untangling concepts like emotions, feelings and states, not just in theory, but through your own 'insperience' of each.   Once again practising almost any kind of meditation will take you down this path.   That, combined with contemplating your emotions, feelings and states will serve to awaken your awareness of exactly what these words and concepts really mean to you, within the reality of... YOU!

So here, to help you on your way, are some clues around these three frequent creations of our consciousness. Starting with STATE.

State of Being

The being that we are is conscious and aware. As you will have noticed I often use the word 'consciousness' to describe the being that 'I am'.   Sometimes we say to someone who is in a panic or racked with anxiety, "You are in a right old state, aren't you?". Which is another way of saying, "You seem intensely emotionally upset about something!". So we can use the word 'state' in that way. How I generally use it is not to describe an emotional disturbance but to describe the 'core states' of every being, prior to any emotion; states of being such as love, peace and joy.   These are more 'stable' states of consciousness, free of the disturbance of emotion, prior to any and all attachment.

In a loving 'state', when you are being loving, then you are in your most natural state of consciousness. You are at peace within your self and giving of your energy.   Similarly when we use the word peace, and you are in a peaceful state within your being, you are in your most natural state. And when you are joyful, it's not an excited joy, or an extroverted joy. That's excitement and extroversion, and true joy is not excitement. It's quiet, like a subtle song singing in your heart. The soul is dancing lightly to the tune of the heart, so to speak! In that 'joyful state' of being you are being your most natural. You 'feel' that state when you are in it. But only because there is no emotion in the way! It's not easy, at first, to discern the moments in which you are 'feeling' a natural state of being and in which moments you are feeling some emotion. Gradually however, with the practice of meditation and contemplation it becomes clearer.

There is one major challenge within all this. We have forgotten the true meaning of love. When we use the word 'love', most of the time we really mean 'attachment' and 'emotion'. And that throws a spanner into the work of self-understanding. So it is slightly essential that we hunt down the true meaning of love at some stage in our life. Otherwise we may miss knowing it completely, as I suspect many do.

Good Vibrations

When your consciousness is in those 'states' of peace, love or joy, it is simply the energy of YOU vibrating at a certain frequency. As you do you will 'feel' it first your self. As you do you will be able to adapt that vibration/feeling at will. For example when you are in a loving state of being you will be able to adapt that energy of love into perhaps compassion for one person or caring for another or patience towards another. So you FEEL the STATE you are in and you can alter your feeling at will within that state.

But to do that, to stay in those states, to be able to alter your feelings, to adjust the way you use the energy of you, then you need to remain free within your consciousness. Free in this sense means non-attached. As soon as you attach your self to something (some thing) then you are no longer free. Then, if whatever you are attached to is damaged or threatened in any way that's when you lose that core state of being and you generate a disturbance within you called emotion. The three main emotions in all our lives are fear, anger and sadness. When you are creating and feeling any of these emotions you are no longer in a 'core state' of being. Your being is in a sorry state! That means an emotional state. The main 'families of emotion' are sadness, anger and fear. As we explore their many forms the main causes of each are also revealed.

SADNESS

Sadness is what we usually call unhappiness. It always follows the belief that we have lost something. Sometimes we imagine we are going to lose something and we make our self feel sad in advance! Sadness must follow, be a consequence, of the belief in possession and ownership. We are attached to the belief that things and people are MINE! Then we are attached to the actual things and people! So that means sadness, i.e. unhappiness, will be inevitable. This is why, as soon as you search for happiness, you are guaranteed to suffer from unhappiness. That's because we seek happiness outside of our self in things and people, believing that 'when they are mine I will be happy'. But the truth is nothing is ever mine because everything comes and goes. That's a fact of life. This is why 'pursuing' happiness is always destined to end in tears.

The emotion of sadness has many faces.

Melancholy – listen to most modern music, especially love songs, and you will hear strains of melancholy threaded through the melody. Often some specific loss is mentioned in the lyrics. In some songs sadness replaces love. Love is sung about in a melancholic way! This truly is emotional confusion!

Depression – after many moments of sadness, after creating many memories of sadness, a deep almost permanent habit of heaviness sets in our consciousness, which we call depression.

Disappointment – this is the sadness that usually follows the belief that we have been let down. Until we realize the other is not responsible for our emotion of sadness we will always believe others make us feel sad. Only then are we able to stay calm and contented when they don't do what they say.

Sentimentality – is a form of pining for what was! A nostalgic look back at what was and a longing for what is now no longer! It is a frequent companion of nostalgia, which is attachment to memories of a past that has obviously gone!

Hopelessness – is the result of believing that I have lost so much already and there is going to be more uncontrollable loss in the future, so what's the point of making any effort in any context.

Helplessness – is the result of remembering I could do nothing to stop any loss in the past and that the same is likely to happen in the future

FEAR

Fear is always the fear of 'future' loss. It is never the fear of the unknown. You cannot fear what you do not know. It is ALWAYS the fear that you are going to lose what you know or what you believe you have. If it's not tangible things we fear losing, it's intangible things. You may fear a loss of your comfort zone. Maybe someone threw this book away after the first chapter because they feared losing the beliefs that they are attached to by being open to the insights here!

Fear takes many 'emotional forms' prior to finding expression in our behavior. Here are a few.

Anxiety – is fearfulness about something that may be lost any minute now! Sometimes we just cannot see what we are anxious about. It's just become a habit to create anxiety wherever we are.

Tension – is similar to anxiety. There is tension in both playing and watching the game because the match may be lost.

Worry – is the classic misuse of our imagination as we visualize the future loss of something or someone or even our own life. We then use that image of future loss to distort the energy of our consciousness from love into fear.

Panic – a panic attack is usually based on the fear of the immediate arrival of fear and the loss of our comfort! That's the result of creating fear habitually over a long period of time.

Terror – is extreme fear associated with what is imagined to be the immanent and cruel loss of life itself.

ANGER

Anger is the disturbance that we create when we believe someone else is to blame for our loss in the past, or that stands in the way of our desires and will therefore be responsible for our imagined loss in the future! Anger usually follows sadness as we project our suffering onto another person or an event, both of which we cannot control. Anger is the currency of conflict.

It has many faces including:

Irritation – this is anger taking birth. Something is not quite or exactly as it should be according to 'me', and it's starting to be bothersome!

Frustration – usually arises when things are not going exactly as you are trying to make them, people are not doing exactly as you direct them.

Resentment – is when we hold onto a simmering angriness from a previous event or encounter where we 'believe' we were hurt or affected by another.

Rage – is obviously the most extreme form of anger and usually the most violent when it is brought through into behavior.

Annoyance, Grumpiness, Fury, Wrath, Hostility, Bitterness, Spite, Loathing, Hate and **Scorn** all contain anger as their main ingredient.

All forms of anger arise from the belief that 'I am not getting or keeping what I want'. That is then translated in our heads as 'you are responsible for my unhappiness therefore you have hurt me'. Which of course is not true. No one hurts you ever! They may hurt your body perhaps, but not YOU. They hurt your ego perhaps, but not YOU! Only the realization of that inner reality can free us from being infected by the current global emotional contagion of sadness, angriness and fearfulness.

Then there are the 'emotional mixes' that constitute some of our most common disturbances:

Envy – is a mix of sadness and resentment (anger). I want what you have and I am upset that I am not getting it and that you have it.

Guilt – is a mix of sadness, anger and fear. I believe I have done something wrong and I am therefore bad, so I am *sad* at losing my self-image based on 'I am good!' I then become *angry* with myself for doing so. And I *fear* someone will find out and then I will lose my reputation in the eyes of others.

Shame – is similar to guilt, but is mostly a mix of sadness and fear around the loss of reputation and the fear of what others will think.

Hurt – is a mix of sadness and anger again; sadness at the loss of a comfort zone or reputation, and anger at whoever is perceived to be responsible. 'You hurt my feelings' is a classic illusion we create when we don't realize we are the sole creators of our emotions.

Embarrassment - is a mix of sadness from loss of face/reputation, and that fear that people will see and remember, all of which easily turns to anger at the person perceived to be responsible.

Despair – is also a mix of sadness and fear; sadness of the loss we call failure and the debilitating fear that it is going to continue.

Remember, you 'will feel' each of these emotions as they arise, as you create them. But no one else is responsible for their creation. While each of these emotions is flaring in your consciousness you will be unable to choose and change what you feel. Only when the emotion 'dies down', and is no longer present in your consciousness, can you choose and change your feelings. The more self-aware you become the more you will see, feel and know this for your self.

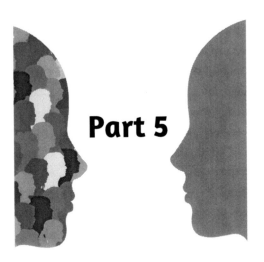

Part 5

Renewing Your Energy

Why our attempts to break the law are
exhausting us ON the Way!

The Lawfulness of Consciousness!

You have energy because you are energy. As we have been reminding ourselves the energy of consciousness is what I/you/we all are. While your body can lose energy, and you sometimes have feelings of being physically run down, YOU cannot lose energy because you cannot lose your self. All of you is always there, which is here!

However we do sometimes feel what we sometimes call mental and emotional exhaustion. Not because we lose energy, but because the 'energy of me' is blocked and distorted by the habits of attachment and ego. We then distort, which means misuse, our energy by creating emotion. Further exhaustion ensues. That's why we usually need a rest after any intense emotional outburst or flaring. If only because emotions eventually affect the energy of our body.

Being mentally tired, which is sometimes called laziness; being on edge and reactive towards others, which is sometimes called grumpiness; being unenthusiastic and vacant of all vitality, which is sometimes called boredom; are some of many signs that our energy is 'locked' and made deviant by old patterns and habits of attaching and emoting. It's as if we put our self in a kind of drowsy state and start sleep-walking our way through life. But we just don't notice. Until perhaps we bump into someone that we recognize is more awake and their energy is consistently enthusiastic and bright, warm and vital. We then wonder why we are not the same!

It's the Law!

The reason that we feel and believe our energy is depleting is we are trying hard, but unknowingly, to break the laws of consciousness. These are the spiritual laws that arise from our natural state of being, which is enthusiastic and loving, peaceful and content. While nation states create the laws of the land it is our 'natural states of being' that generate the laws of human consciousness - otherwise known as spiritual laws. To realign and renew the energy of our being, the energy of the 'self', we need to be aware of why and how we are inclined to act against these spiritual laws and gently correct those inclinations.

ALL human made laws throughout the world, regardless of history, culture or context, exist because we are attempting to break the laws of consciousness. These spiritual laws 'ultimately' cannot be broken. It's our repeated attempts to break them that lies at the heart of all human suffering and conflict, disorder and chaos. Nevertheless, we all persistently keep attempting to break the laws of our own consciousness, without knowing that we are trying do so! The creation of any attachment and the consequent ego is in itself an attempt to break such laws. It tends to take us some time to recognize our own consistent failure, and stop attempting! It usually depends on the frequency and intensity of our suffering and how much unhappiness we are able to tolerate!

The Laws of the Land
We live by what we call the laws of the land. At least most of us do, most of the time! The purpose of those laws is to maintain order and harmony within the collective that we call 'society'. Each year seems to see an increase in 'law-making' either in an attempt to control an increasingly unruly population or, in the minds of the conspiracy theorists, *it's 'the few' trying to gain greater control of the behavior of 'the many*! Certainly there does seem to be a slow and inexorable increase in disorder and disharmony within many

societies throughout the world. Such is the nature of entropy! If there still existed a 'natural' order and harmony between us all as individuals, and between the populations of different countries and communities, there would be no need to create and enforce any laws. So far so obvious!

Peaceful Incarceration!

If you break one of society's laws the consequence will be some form of punishment. You will be made to suffer if you are caught. Unless of course you are enlightened enough to have fully realized the cause of any suffering is not external (Parts One and Two of this book), and you are internally powerful enough to maintain your inner peace and contentment during incarceration! If you were that enlightened you would probably be less likely to break a law in the first place. It is the correlation between law-breaking and suffering that we are interested in, as we proceed to nature's laws.

Natural Laws

The natural world around us has it's own laws that maintain balance, order and harmony. These laws are 'built in' to the substance of nature's many forms and interconnected systems. The most obvious natural law is the one that keeps you in your seat right now - the law of gravity. If you thought, for a moment, that you could break the law of gravity, went to the top of the building and jumped off to prove that you could fly, in about two and a half seconds you would experience much physical pain, if you were still conscious!

Note the correlation again between pain and attempted law-breaking. As we will see, all human suffering, at whatever level, is the result of an attempt to break a law somewhere in the physical, mental or spiritual universe.

Are You Coal or Diamond?

Staying in the physical universe, take a lump of coal. As you look at the coal all you can see is a black, dirty, ragged edged piece of material - a lump of physical matter that crumbles easily. As you may have learned in your physics or chemistry class at school, over time, this ugly piece of matter will become beautiful, at least to human eyes. Many of us were taught that diamonds come from coal. But they don't. It's too great a transformation. But what they both have in common is carbon. They have different carbon structures.

The carbon structures of diamonds are shaped deep below ground as a result of two prevailing physical laws that exist within the underground environment. The first law is gravity, which means huge amounts of pressure will be applied to the carbon atoms. The second law is that of thermodynamics, or heat exchange. Over a long period of time these two 'natural laws' will transform the structure of the carbon into a rock, harder than all other rocks. We value diamonds so highly we give them the status of the most precious stone in the world. Suddenly, from a lump of carbon matter we have a pure, transparent, extremely hard, priceless piece of material. It is able to cut all other solid substances while splitting pure white light into all the colors of the spectrum. Such is the ultimate power of the natural laws within the natural world to 'transform' the material of the physical world.

Using those two forms of carbon as a metaphor for consciousness, would you say your consciousness, which is you, is more like a lump of coal - rough, dark, dusty, fragile and dirty, or is it more like a diamond - transparent, clean, sharp and extremely stable, strong and durable? Most of us would probably have to admit we are more like the coal – a little stressed, thinking negative and sometimes dark thoughts, a bit fragile which means sensitive to others comments, probably a bit rough around the edges and emotionally unstable! Not necessarily in that order!

The Spiritual Laws

In society laws are made by people. In the natural physical world the laws are already built in to nature. Within consciousness, spiritual laws are also 'built in'. But they need to be restored to our awareness and activated every day if we are to be and live according to our true nature. So what are the specific spiritual laws, which already exist within the inner environment of our consciousness, that will transform our consciousness from a coal like state into a diamond like state, i.e. into a transparent, stable, powerful, durable and beautiful state? What are the spiritual laws that we are unknowingly attempting to break, thereby ensuring our consciousness remains more coal-like? And how are we to know when we are trying to break such laws? What are the signs?

Awareness is the Key

Before we identify and explore each law and its transformative effect, a word about 'awareness'. When you are 'in harmony' with each law then you will be in a certain 'state of awareness', and all will be well 'within you'. You will also be seen and felt by others to be calm and peaceful, recognized by others to be open and honest, appreciated by others for your loving and compassionate nature. That means there will be a natural order and harmony within you the conscious being. You will 'feel' your self to be at peace, to be content and loving towards others! But if you attempt to break any of the laws of consciousness then you will lose that 'awareness'. Disorder and chaos will reign 'within' you, and you will 'feel' peaceless, possibly sorrowful, certainly fearful and probably irritated with others and with life around you. Those are the classic symptoms of 'suffering' and they are also the signs that you are attempting to break a spiritual law.

Revealing the Spiritual Laws to Your Self

This is where things become a little deeper and even more subtle. As we explore the spiritual laws of consciousness we will identify the exact awareness that tells you whether you are in harmony with each spiritual law. Each 'law', and its corresponding 'awareness', is worthy of contemplation. Only then will you 'see and realize' for your self. Otherwise it's just more ideas on the page which sound interesting/insightful/useful, but they won't make much difference to the way you are, or the way you live, or the way you feel, until you see/realize for your self.

If we pollute the physical atmosphere of the world it is an act that despoils the natural harmonious state of the natural world. It is, in a sense, an act against the laws that maintain harmony in nature. Nature will eventually let us know by creating disharmony in the form of extreme disturbances in its weather patterns or the breakdown of some parts of the ecosystem. Similarly, within our consciousness, if we pollute our natural state of consciousness, in other words if we attach our self, and identify our self, with something we are not, then our nature will let us know by creating internal disharmony in the form of a disturbance called emotion.

As we explore the laws of spirit we will see what we unknowingly do to try to break the law and the specific influence of the ego. We will identify the exact nature of the 'emotional feedback' that we will receive from within our own being as we attempt to break each law. As you move slowly through each law, and the awareness that signifies you are in harmony with the law, allow time for contemplation in order to see for your self. There are seven primary 'laws of consciousness' that exist within the spiritual being that you are: the laws of time, purpose, identity, silence, peace, love, happiness. First, we identify the 'awareness' that corresponds to each law.

Are YOU a Law Breaker or Law Maker?

1 The Spiritual LAW of TIME

When you are in harmony with the Law of Time you will be AWARE of your own 'ETERNITY'.

You will be aware of your self as an eternal being, beyond the passing of time that is symbolized by changes in the material world around you, and on the face of those clever little measuring machines called clocks! You would be aware of the transience of everything and everyone around you, while being aware of the permanence of your self, the 'I' that says, 'I am'. This awareness, which is restored through the practice of meditation, becomes 'real' when there is self-realization. The challenge of course, is to maintain this awareness in our day-to-day life, moment-by-moment, in the world.

2 The Spiritual LAW of PURPOSE

When you are in harmony with the Law of Purpose you will be AWARE that you are here as a creator to be CREATIVE.

You will be aware of yourself as a 'master creator'. You will be aware that the core purpose of living in this world, which is your relationship with matter and other embodied souls, is to be creative. You will be aware that you are here to create your life in the dimensions of time, space and matter. Just as the seed of a flower is dormant until it is placed in the soil, it's as if we are dormant beings of spiritual energy until we occupy and animate the form of our body. Once in the soil the seed then creates and expresses (presses out) its form and fragrance, which it shares with the world as it becomes a flower. Similarly we 'create' our character and then share the fragrance of our personality with those around us through the material form we call the body. We also get to 'play' with matter, other than our body, and in so doing we create and co-create our life. This is not so easy to realize if we have been conditioned out of our awareness as creators and into the mindset of being producers/consumers, as most of us have.

Before moving to the next page go down column 2 below, take some moments to reflect and see if you can 'see' what would be your 'awareness' when you are 'in harmony' with each of the other five spiritual laws. Then go to the next page and see if we agree!

Spiritual Law	Awareness
Law of **TIME**	Awareness of your own ETERNITY
Law of **PURPOSE**	Awareness that I am here to CREATE
Law of **IDENTITY**	Awareness of
Law of **SILENCE**	Awareness of my
Law of **LOVE**	Awareness of
Law of **PEACE**	Awareness of
Law of **HAPPINESS**	Awareness of

3 The Spiritual LAW of IDENTITY

When you are in harmony with the Law of Identity YOU will be AWARE of your self as the 'I' that says 'I am', i.e. a BEING with no worldly identity.

Your sense of identity will not be based on your body or on any of the material labels that we give to our body like nationality, race, religion, class, gender etc. You will be aware of your self as a being of consciousness that is animating the form/body that you occupy. While you would create an identity, and perhaps several identities, for the purpose of interacting with others in the world, you would be aware that any such identity would not be you! You would therefore be egoless. You would be able to 'play with' such 'worldly' identities to operate in the world. But within your self you would be fully aware of your inner freedom as someone with no intrinsic identity!

4 The Spiritual LAW of SILENCE

When you are in harmony with the Law of Silence you will be AWARE of your unlimited and infinite POWER.

You will be aware of your self as pure, concentrated energy. You wouldn't 'think it', but just be aware of it! In your relationship with the material world you will be aware of your capacity to use your inner power to manifest your life in the world. However, you will also be in a desireless state having realized you are not dependent on the material energies of the world for your state of being. You will be able to still your mind at will. All memories would be merged within you and yet accessible at will. Nothing outside your self would be able to randomly trigger them into your consciousness. You will be aware that whatever 'arises' within you is shaped by the reality of your true underlying nature, which is infinitely peaceful and an unlimited source of love.

5 The Spiritual LAW of PEACE

When you are in harmony with the Law of Peace you will be AWARE of your PURITY.

Purity does not mean being puritanical. Purity means you will be aware of your absolute clarity as you use the inner eye of your intellect to discern reality from illusion, the authentic from the inauthentic. You will immediately see through anything that is false, both in the intentions and behaviors of others, and within the world itself. You will be untouchable and therefore undisturbable by anything happening around you, while being able to respond benevolently towards everyone who meets you.

6 The Spiritual LAW OF LOVE

When you are in harmony with the Law of Love you will be AWARE of the unbreakable UNITY of all things on all levels at all times, despite 'apparent' fragmentation and separation.

Where there is the light of love there is union or unity. When you are aware of the UNITY of all and every thing, 'the all' is held and seen within consciousness as One. There is an awareness of the Oneness of everything throughout space and throughout time. You are aware of your intimate connection to 'the all'.

7 The Spiritual LAW of HAPPINESS

When you are in harmony with the Law of Happiness you will be AWARE of your FREEDOM.

You will truly sense you are a free spirit without burden or barrier, without limitation or constraint. You will not think 'I am free', you will simply be the embodiment of freedom – open, unpretentious and transparent. The purest joy arises naturally from the heart of your being.

Spiritual Law	Awareness
Law of TIME	Awareness of your own ETERNITY
Law of PURPOSE	Awareness that I am here to CREATE
Law of IDENTITY	Awareness of your SELF as SPIRIT or NO ONE!
Law of SILENCE	Awareness of Your POWER
Law of LOVE	Awareness of UNITY / ONENESS
Law of PEACE	Awareness of Your PURITY
Law of HAPPINESS	Awareness of Your FREEDOM

What we do in our attempt to break the laws of spirit

Any sign of suffering, which means any form or level of unhappiness, are signals that you are trying to break one or many natural spiritual laws of consciousness. Each and every day you will do many things that demonstrate you are attempting to break each and usually all the spiritual laws! For example:

1 The Spiritual LAW of TIME

When you are in harmony with the Law of Time then YOU will be AWARE of your own 'ETERNITY'.

But what do you do many times each day that demonstrates you have lost your awareness of your own eternity and are therefore trying to 'break the law'?

You look at your watch and believe that it is telling you the time! But time is not found on the face of a clock. Clocks are simply ingenious machines we invented in an attempt to measure the space between our experiences, which is essentially the space between perceived events in the world. To a being in their natural timeless awareness, the use of clock time is just a convenient tool to organize one's attention and energy in the context of one's corporeal relationships and tasks during each day!

What does the EGO say in order to get you to try to break the law of time?

It says, "Hurry up or you will run out of time (attachment to the image of getting stuff done by a certain clock time). If you can do this faster you will save time (attachment to the idea of having more time for other things). There will be more time tomorrow, so leave it till then (attachment to the idea that I can/should do something else in this moment now)."

What do you FEEL as a result?

The emotion of fear in the form of feelings of being rushed, stressed, pressured, panic.

Remember, any sign of (mental/emotional) suffering or discomfort is a sign that you are attempting to break a spiritual law that exists within you. Why? Your true nature defines the laws of spirit and your true nature is peaceful, stable, loving and joyful. Your true nature is fearless, sadless and angerless... so to speak! We all learn to act against our nature, which is to attempt to break the law. Creating the EGO (attachment to and identification with a mental image) is the 'primary act' against the true nature of your consciousness. It is 'the' mistake we all learn to make. Hence the feeling of discomfort and suffering (emotion) which is the signal that you are attempting to break a spiritual law (an act against your nature). It is telling you that you have lost your ability to be your self and there is therefore a loss of awareness of your own eternity.

2 The Spiritual LAW of PURPOSE

When you are in harmony with the Law of Purpose you will be AWARE of your CREATIVE capacity.

But what do you do many times each day, which demonstrates that you have lost the awareness of your creative capacity?

You will be 'impressed' by others creativity. You bow down to their creativity and you absorb their creation. You may even worship/idolize what has been created by others. You will allow others creations to influence your state of being and therefore your feelings. Going to the cinema and watching TV are the most common ways in which we are impressed by, and bow down to, the creativity of others, and then we use their ideas and images to shape our self and dictate the emotions that we feel.

What does the EGO say in order to get you to try to break the law?

It generates thoughts and says things like, "I am not creative like them. I could not do that. I am not good enough. They are so great, unlike me. Oooh, isn't that so amazing, that's awesome!".

And what do you FEEL as a result?

Inadequate, smallness, low self-worth, incapable. You will generate and feel the emotions of sadness (at the loss of self value), and frustration (at being less than others) and anxiety (that it may continue).

The secret here is 'don't be impressed' by anything or anyone. When you are impressed you are 'taking from' whatever you allow to impress you. In such moments you take 'their' creation and use it to shape your consciousness as you attach your self to their creation in your own mind. When you have awoken to who you really are, when you fully realize your own creative capacity, you 'appreciate and applaud' others creation so that you are 'giving to' their creation. In such moments you are the master of your consciousness as you 'create' and distribute the energy of you in the form of appreciation and blessings. Can you see the difference?

Take a few moments to reflect on your own experiences and see if you can fill in the other five on the next page in a similar way.

1 Spiritual Law	2 Awareness	3 What we do in our attempt to break the law	4 Why we try to break the law	5 What we 'feel' when we try to break the law
Law of Time	Awareness of your own ETERNITY	Look at your watch and keep checking the time	Ego gives rise to the illusion that time is running out, you might lose time but if you hurry you could save time!	Rushed, panicked, stressed
Law of Purpose	Awareness that I am here to CREATE	Admire, absorb and bow down to the creation of others e.g. entertainment	Ego gives rise to the illusion that... I am not creative	Small, inadequate incapable, and low self-esteem
Law of Identity	Awareness of your SELF as SPIRIT		Ego gives rise to the illusion that...	
Law of Silence	Awareness of Your POWER		Ego gives rise to the illusion that...	
Law of Love	Awareness of UNITY		Ego gives rise to the illusion that...	
Law of Peace	Awareness of Your PURITY		Ego gives rise to the illusion that...	
Law of Happiness	Awareness of Your FREEDON		Ego gives rise to the illusion that...	

3   The Spiritual LAW of IDENTITY

When you are in harmony with the Law of Identity YOU will be AWARE of your self only as the 'I' that says 'I am', a BEING with no worldly identity. Pure awareness itself!

But what do you do many times a day that demonstrates you are attempting to break the law of identity?

You look at the reflection of the body that you occupy in a mirror, believing that it is you. You paint it, cream it, nip it, tuck it, slim it, (well maybe not too many times a day!) believing that you are taking care of your self. You worry about how your physical appearance looks in the eyes of others. You become 'body conscious'.

And what does the EGO say in order to encourage you to break the law?

It says things like "I am this body. I am not a very good-looking body. I need to do something with or to this physical appearance to feel better. I need to make me look more beautiful by dressing/decorating/building my body." All are forms of attachment to, and identification with, the form that we occupy and animate. This is the origin of all other attachments and faces of the ego.

And what do you FEEL as a result?

Low self-esteem, insecure, anxiety and perhaps a fluctuating self-loathing. The emotions of sadness (at the loss of looks/beauty) and fear (at the prospect of continuing decay and inevitable death!) will arise as you believe you are losing your 'looks', vigour or health.

Your body might be losing something, but YOU are not!

4 The Spiritual LAW of SILENCE

When you are in harmony with the Law of Silence you will be AWARE of your unlimited and infinite POWER.

But what do you do many times each day that demonstrates you are attempting to break the Law of Silence?

You think too much and you think thoughts that are contrary to your true nature. The noise of thought masks and dissipates the power of your silence. The busyness of your mind masks the stillness at the core of your being. Thinking too much is one of the signs of overstimulation. As we receive the world around us through our senses we create too many unnecessary thoughts about what is going on 'out there'.   When we believe we are just a body we see our self as small against the backdrop of that big world full of media magnified people 'out there'. So we start to think thoughts about our self and how deficient and incapable we are compared to 'them'. We feel far from powerful. Even those who talk and look as if they are confident, capable and powerful are usually thinking similar thoughts internally, behind their mask. They are either good at disguising it or they are trying so hard to make an impression on others in the world believing it to be the route to success and happiness. They are trying to be somebody! We all tend to learn that it's important to try to 'be somebody'. But we don't notice that that's usually the moment we start forgetting how to be our self!

It all leads to unnatural feelings of limitation and inadequacy, feelings of powerlessness and helplessness. Hence the efficacy of some form of spiritual practice and spiritual study. These practices slow and deepen your thinking and feeling. They re-awaken the truth and the beauty of you. Gradually you start to draw on your inner resources, your inner power, as you break your dependence on external sources of stimulation. Eventually you will master your consciousness enough to be still and silent. It cannot be done by force. Only by realizing that while you may be 'in' this physical body, 'in' this material world, you are not 'of' this world!

So why do we frequently lose our awareness of our infinite power?

Because the EGO says, "I need to think about this. This is a worry... this needs thinking through... I'm not sure about this... this could have negative implications in my life...I need to be more, do more, achieve more...than this". And many other thought patterns, which then trigger the creation of emotion.

And what do you FEEL – doubtful, mentally tired, frustrated, uncertain, weakened. The emotions of sadness (at the loss of the ability to respond with an open and unlimited attitude), and frustration (at the inability to be clear and decisive) will always be in the background.

5 The Spiritual LAW of PEACE

When you are in harmony with the Law of Peace you will be AWARE of your PURITY.

But what do you do many times each day, which demonstrates you are attempting to break the Law of Peace? You make your self peaceless by absorbing then recreating violent and dark ideas and images in your mind. Then empowering them to shape your feelings.

Imagine a lake where the water is pure. It is calm, still and clear. You can see deeply into its depths. Then comes the factory on the hill above. The effluent from the factory trickles down the hill and seeps into the water. It starts to become cloudy, perhaps even 'effervescent', as many toxins pollute the water. Purity is lost and the water becomes murky and disturbed. A truly peaceful 'state of being' is pure and has nothing dark or negative within it to cloud consciousness, nothing toxic that upsets your stillness or your ability to concentrate and focus.

But the EGO says, "They are bad people", as it criticizes others. "This is a terrible day", as it complains about the weather. "The violence in this movie is awesome", as we stimulate our consciousness with violent images in the name of relaxation. Our ego both consumes and creates negative images and ideas and, as it does, it pollutes consciousness. Purity of consciousness, and therefore the inner peace of our being, is lost.

And what do you FEEL? Agitated, aggravated and tired, while the emotions of sadness (loss of peace), fear (that our suffering may continue) will strike with daily frequency, and anger will arise as resentment towards others, as we project blame for our unhappiness onto other people in the world around us.

6 The Spiritual LAW OF LOVE

When you are in harmony with the law of love you will be aware of the infinite and unbreakable UNITY of all things on all levels despite the 'apparent' fragmentation and separation.

But what do you do many times a day that demonstrates you are attempting to break the Law of Love?

You become attached to fragments of 'the all'. You see things in a fragmented way. Your perception separates everything and everyone from everything else and everyone else. There is always an 'us' and 'them'. You have the desire to separate your self and be alone in order to avoid others, or be 'only' with someone that you choose.

This vision of unity, this awareness of oneness, is not easy to restore as all our conditioning has led us away from this perception. We have wandered far from the true meaning of love and a perception arising from a loving state. Instead, we tend to hold the idea of love in association only with exclusive, intimate, romantic but separated relationships. Most of our learned behaviors have their roots in ego and are therefore contrary to a loving state of being and doing, e.g. criticizing, complaining, resenting, ignoring, blaming, rejecting are but a few. Why?

Because the EGO says, "I am separate. I have to be different. I am alone here. They are different and they are separate. They are no good. I am better than them or I am lesser than them. I need to fix them so they don't affect me. I need to be somebody to stand out amongst these manybodies... so to speak!".

And what do you FEEL? Lonely, isolated, fragmented and futility, which means the presence of a sadness at the loss of connection; anger when others reciprocate your non-acceptance of them and they don't accept you; fear that this may continue and that you may always be separate and alone, even when you are in a crowd!

7 The Spiritual LAW of HAPPINESS

When you are in harmony with the Law of Happiness you will be AWARE of your absolute FREEDOM.

But what do you do many times a day that demonstrates you are attempting to break the Law of Happiness?
You become attached to the images of things, people and places and memories in your mind. As we have seen all attachment leads to some kind of suffering which is unhappiness. When you are attached to anything or anyone you are essentially 'trapped in' what

you are attached to. Then we point the finger of blame at others for what we feel when what we are attached to is threatened or removed.

The EGO says, "You need and must have that. You need them and must be with them. You are mine. That is mime. That will be mine and in the meantime I will act as if it is mine!'"

And what do you FEEL? Enslaved, trapped, victimized, sometimes persecuted and frequently threatened. Even when you have accumulated a lot of material stuff you still feel an inner emptiness. There will be frequent moments of *sadness* as you lose your freedom to what you believe you possess, but you may not make the connection! Frequent bouts of *anger* at the actions of others whom you perceive to be responsible for denying you what you want or that you think are responsible for any loss. And *fear* that all that you have become attached to and dependent on will be taken away or lost. All are popular forms of unhappiness!

These spiritual laws exist within the consciousness of every human being. They arise from our original and natural state of being. They are our natural state of being. All our societal laws become necessary only because we have forgotten how to be our true and natural self. When we violate these spiritual laws we create violence within our self. This then finds its way out into our interactions with each other. Hence the need for laws within society to maintain peace and harmony between people.

In the world, laws are made and enforced *by the state*. In consciousness, laws arise naturally *from your state* (of being). In both cases laws are broken when we either forget something or want something badly enough. The reward for breaking the laws of society and the laws of consciousness will be the same. Suffering in one of its many guises.

1 Spiritual Law	2 Awareness	3 What we do in our attempt to break the law	4 Why we try to break the law	5 The Emotions that we 'Feel' when we try to break the law
Law of Time	Awareness of your own ETERNITY	Look at your watch and keep checking the time	Ego gives rise to the illusion that...time is running out, you might lose time but if you hurry you could save time	Rushed, panicked, stressed
Law of Purpose	Awareness that I am here to CREATE	Admire, absorb and bow down to the creation of others e.g. entertainment	Ego gives rise to the illusion that... I am not creative	Small, inadequate and low self esteem
Law of Identity	Awareness of your SELF as SPIRIT	Look in the mirror and believe you are what you see - decorate your body!	Ego gives rise to the illusion that... I am just a body	Anxiety (ageing), worry (what other might think of you) low self worth
Law of Silence	Awareness of Your POWER	Think too much, over think, analytical thinking	Ego gives rise to the illusion that... I need to think about this	Tiring, futility, confusion
Law of Love	Awareness of UNITY	Separate our self -	Ego gives rise to the illusion that... I need to be alone!	Isolation, loneliness
Law of Peace	Awareness of Your PURITY	Absorb and create dark and violent ideas and images	Ego gives rise to the illusion that... It's relaxing, it's relieving, it's entertaining	Agitated, exhausted and peaceless
Law of Happiness	Awareness of Your FREEDOM	Blame others for what we feel. Become attached to...anything	Ego gives rise to the illusion that... They are responsible for my feelings. That's mine, they are mine	Trapped, enslaved, fearful of loss

Simply a Description of You!

For many, the process of seeing and understanding how 'spiritual law' originates within 'the self' can be a little too subtle and perhaps a little too... complex! But if you can glimpse each of the above aspects of consciousness you may then see that each of these laws is ultimately not separate within you. We only separate them out here in order to explain and perceive. They are like a matrix within our being. They are all connected. They are all variations of the vibration we can each create within the energy of our consciousness. When seen as such you may get a glimpse of your own beauty at this, the deepest spiritual level. They are like strands within your consciousness that form the tapestry of the inner beauty of your being.

As you enhance your ability to see all the connections and implications of each law through practices such as meditation and contemplation, try occasionally resting your attention on what it all reveals. It leaves you with both an essenceful and yet spiritual description of your self, a subtle but simple profile of your self, which you can then use to remind your self of your... true self. It paints a picture of the spiritual beauty that you bring to this world.

From the laws of spirit come the following short spiritual affirmations. Put them on a page in your notebook or diary and then drop in occasionally to remind your self about your true self, using the following:

I am eternal	I am a creator	I am spirit
I am infinite	I am power	I am peace
I am connected	I am love	I am free
I am contentment	I am light	I am awareness

Yes, they are just words and words can only point. They point towards a state of being, a state of consciousness that is an aspect of your true nature as a being of spiritual energy. If you go in the direction in which they point, which is to your self, and then see if you can create and 'be in' these states you will likely find that when you do you will not be able to maintain them for too long at first. At which point, if you are interested, you will likely ask your self why? And the next question will be what's stopping me from 'being in' and knowing these states? What's IN the way'?

You are a scientist and the laboratory is your consciousness. You are conducting experiments around what happens when you follow the signposts represented by the above words, by the above 'I AMs'!

Mix them up, find the best order, play with them, ask your self what do they mean to me? Notice when you feel contrary to any of them, then go hunting for the attachment, for the particular face of the ego, that is sabotaging your state of being.

Patiently allow these original and eternal characteristics of the authentic you to come alive as states of awareness within you. Be careful however, that you don't just create concepts about them and then identify with the concepts! That would then be the ego pulling another of its hijack stunts!

Your State of Trueness

Spiritual laws arise from your true, original and eternal state of being, which existed before it was infected by the virus of attachment, and the birth of our old and toxic companion, the ego. Spiritual laws exist within you and arise from you! They describe the true you. They are your truth. When you are in your natural state of being which is peaceful, loving and content, you are in what you could call your state of 'trueness'. This is why 'truth' is a state of being and not a set of words, ideas, theories or philosophies.

Truth is that which never changes, that which is eternal. That's you again! Not your personality, that's your creation, and it changes, but the 'you' that is prior to thoughts and feelings, memories and perceptions.

While your state of being changes in it's vibration, which means your thoughts and feelings change, you don't. That sounds like a contradiction. Let's do it again. While your states of being can change, you don't. You are the being. So you would think that you change. Well you do and yet you don't! What never changes is your capacity to be in your highest state. And it's as if that highest state, which is also your original state, always exists within you! This capacity to be in your highest or purist state can never be taken from you. In other words, that cannot change. Just as you are the being that can create any state, you are the being that has the capacity.

States of being may change but your capacity, which is essentially you, doesn't. So in one sense you are both you and your capacity!

Think of a sponge. It starts out clean, you could say pure, you would definitely say empty, apart from itself! It has tremendous capacity. As you clean anything from a kitchen top to a car, it picks up and becomes full of liquid and all the various substances, germs and bacteria in the dirt it has absorbed. So it loses its cleanliness and its purity. If the sponge had self-awareness and could think, it might even think, "I am full of _ _ _ _!"

Imagine the sponge does have self-awareness, for a moment! When it is full of... stuff, it forgets it is a sponge and it loses awareness of its capacity. Instead it starts to think it IS the stuff that it has absorbed. In essence it learns to believe it is the rubbish that it has gathered as it wiped it's way along the tabletop or the roof of the car or the kitchen floor. Effectively the sponge will have an identity crisis! Well I am sure you know where I am going with this!

The Capacity of Emptiness
Then you clean the sponge by holding it under a flow of running water. Then you let it sit and as it dries out it becomes both clean and empty as it returns to its pure and natural state. It is almost weightless as new sponges are, and so it is a free sponge again... so to speak! It is a sponge with great capacity, which is defined by its emptiness. It is a sponge AND it is its own capacity.

This is a perfect metaphor for consciousness, for you and me. In our pure and natural state we are clean and empty of all and anything toxic. We are attached to nothing. We have no ego because we are not identifying with anything that we are not. There no memories of sadness and fear, hurt and pain. We are empty, yet so light! But with a tremendous capacity to absorb whatever experiences we create as we encounter and interact with others and with the world. Unfortunately we absorb the sights and sounds of the world and we memorize our creations in response to the world. We keep absorbing without releasing, without cleaning, without emptying our self. Our capacity is not only used up, it is being used to 'hold on' to ideas, images, memories, habits that are like toxins to the soul. Not only that, we start to cling to those ideas/images and use them to build our sense of self.

Until one fateful day we just cannot take in or hold any more. We become so confused as to who we are; which idea, image, concept should we use to base our sense of self on today, in this moment? Maybe this one, perhaps that one! We develop our own identity crisis as we jump between multiple identities and it drives us crazy. Suddenly, within our identity crisis, we also feel a kind of emptiness, despite our consciousness being filled and holding onto so much... stuff! While we feel this kind of emptiness we just can't take in, tolerate or process any more!

Empty Equals Full!
It's a paradox to our rational minds that in order to restore our sense of completeness, our fullness, we need to empty our self! We need to cleanse and free our self from all that we have gathered, all the memories and experiences, in order to restore our capacity, and therefore rediscover and recover 'who I really am'!

Then one day, after some inner cleansing, we have a realization. I am simply consciousness itself. I have no worldly identity. My body does, but 'I' don't! I am both creativity and capacity itself. Gradually, as we empty our self, just like that sponge, that capacity is restored and we also restore our awareness of our true inner state known as an 'unlimited consciousness'.

We are 'consciousness' and we are our 'capacity'. They are one and the same and yet, neither is ever lost, only temporarily occupied! That is an eternal truth about your self, which you can know for your self.

IN the Way

What gets in the way of seeing and realizing this is of course our old friend the ego, which is based on the habit of attachment. But you cannot be free of the habit of attaching until you see and realize where you become attached (in your mind) how you become attached (by losing your self in what's on your mind) and why you become attached.

Looking in the Wrong Place

So why do you become attached to anything or anyone? It's just a mistake that occurs as a result of your search for love and happiness, which is to search for your self! You are seeking your self 'out there', you are seeking 'out there' what you believe you have lost, namely love and happiness, without realizing that neither they nor you can ever be found 'out there'! To know your self as you are and be your self as you have always been the search has to end. This paradox will eventually strike everyone who seriously meanders down any authentic spiritual path.

Why do you want, keep, protect and defend anything or anyone? Because you believe they are/it is responsible for your happiness, perhaps even a source of love. It's that false belief, that you 'wiped up' like a sponge, from someone along the way. It's that illusion, and the consequent habits, that run most people's lives today. We can only clean it out of our consciousness when we fully see that all attachment creates insecurity, which is fear and sadness, which is unhappiness. When you see this, fully realize this, it means you have 'seen through' what is IN the way of you being capable of being at peace, of being a source of love for others, and being content at every moment.

What is it like to be in harmony with Spiritual Law?

When you are empty once again, and fully awake and aware of your self as spirit, as soul, which is no one, you won't be thinking that! You will just be that. You will be aware of the lightness of your being as you are no longer attached to, trapped in, any 'thing' within your being. Just as that sponge becomes so much lighter to hold when it's empty, you feel lighter when you are empty, which arises as a feeling of complete fullness or full completeness...or both! But it's what you could call the right kind of fullness, because you feel complete. Words are inadequate to describe. It has to be felt and known. Feeling and knowing are both prior to thought and therefore prior to all description.

No More Mistakes

No longer are you attracted or 'pulled' by something or someone in whom you invest the illusory promise of completion and satisfaction. You now know that completion is being without any attachment or desire whatsoever. In the physical world, we tend to 'add things to', in order to complete something. In the universe of consciousness, in the inner spiritual space that is 'the self', we take away, release and renounce, in order to return to our completion. To become empty is to become full... so to speak!

As you cease to mistake your self for, and trap your self in, something that you are not, you then 'insperience' a natural freedom of being. There is no longer anything else within you that is absorbing the light of you, so you feel the deepest most profound peace, not as just another passing feeling, but as the indestructible core of you. The healing of your misperception of your self as a separate object, plus the restoration of your capacity to transcend the fragmentation of clock time, allows you to perceive the unbreakable unity of all and everything. You 'perceive' the oneness that permeates all life.

You have stopped separating one thing from another or making some things/images more important than others! You notice that everything that is not you is simply an image that passes through your awareness. In that awareness you are capable of holding and embracing 'the all' with ease. As you do it's as if you bestow the most benevolent blessings upon all that you see. You don't think it. No thought is required. You just be it. And as you are being it you are doing it!

Life Comes Through You

You know and feel the deepest contentment because you have stopped judging and trying to fix other people and the world! You recognize that all is as it is meant to be in each and every moment. You feel and know a consistent joyfulness as it surfaces from within your consciousness now that you have ceased trying to attach your heart and take your joy from any 'thing' or person or event. Now you enjoy the company of all others (give your joy) as opposed to being dependent on the presence of a few. You have realized your self to be WHO you truly are, which is, in essence, no one! This allows you to be WHAT you are, a source of love and light in the world without even thinking about it. You are able to see through and dispel the illusion that life is 'happening TO you' as you awaken to the reality that life is NOT happening to you, it's happening THROUGH you!

You are fully aligned and in harmony with the spiritual laws that are the ground of the spiritual being that you are. As that internal harmony flows through you, and from you, it manifests creatively in the relationships and circumstances around you. Your presence has a powerful and deep influence on those who are close to you in the most uplifting ways. Yet, you are also aware that your capacity to touch and uplift those beyond your immediate context is unlimited.

But you don't need to 'think it'.

BUT wait! The moment you attach your self, identify your self, with any 'thing', which means any image or any idea, any memory or any projection, any belief or any concept, then your energy, your light, your vibration, will become trapped and blocked, deviant and distorted. And you will 'feel' it. That's why all distortions and deviations that you see in the world 'out there', otherwise known as violence, have their root cause in this inner mistake we call ego, which is the first distortion, the original deviation, the primary blockage of the energy of our consciousness.

All is Well, All is Well!
Yet... that's also OK! It was and is inevitable. The mistake/s had to happen. It has happened, it is happening, and it will continue to happen, on a grand collective scale. Look at the world 'out there' today and what do you see? Almost continuous conflict, suffering, chaos, imbalance, disharmony; almost everywhere, and almost all the time! Why? It's not right or wrong, or good or bad. It's just the ego at work. It is the accumulation of millions and eventually billions of people making the same single 'mistake' countless times, every day, over centuries.

Now look again through the inner eye that opens when you know your self as the being and not the form. A being that transcends both the *macroscopic* drama of life and all the *microscopic* dramas of men and women. Allow that 'truth' of you as a being of spiritual awareness to inform your perceptions, and lo and behold you will perceive all those human dramas as if they are all still One. They are all part of the same dance, the same play, all ripples across the same ocean, all scenes in the same grand dramatic production, the same epic movie, which is unfolding and enfolding, rising and falling, ebbing and flowing, exactly as it could, as it should, as it will, all around you at every moment!

You are able to perceive all scenes and situations as interconnected threads in the same tapestry of life's rich pageant. You can see that even when all is apparently not well, all is well! For 'the all' is unfolding as it will, as it does, as it is. It is this 'big picture' awareness that also allows you to free yourself from judgment and condemnation, from criticizing and worrying, from controlling and conflicting. In essence, you have made the shifts from resistance to acceptance, from fear to love, from a perception of fragmentation to an awareness of the Oneness of 'the all'.

With your heart cleansed and empty of all animosity and all inclination to attack or defend, from that moment on you know your self as peace, you give of your self as love and others see you as a precious gift in their life.

As you continue to clean and empty your self each day, in a world where we are mostly encouraged to do the opposite, others will see from you that there is a better way, a truer way, a more natural way, a spiritual way, and therefore a happier way, to do life!

To borrow and adapt a well-known aphorism:

Before enlightenment, chopping wood and carrying water.

During enlightenment, cleaning the bucket and sharpening the blade.

After enlightenment, carving the wood into something useful
and offering water to the thirsty!

Part 6

Big Questions

Further Clarity on Ego, Emotions
and the Purpose of Life!

While running a three-day course last year entitled **What's IN the Way IS the Way**, a variety of questions arose from participants. Here are some of those questions and some responses.

How do you stop the ego taking over?

There are many signs and symptoms that indicate we are thinking and acting from a false sense of self. The more you meditate and contemplate on your day-to-day experiences the faster you will become aware of the habitual thoughts and behaviors that arise from the ego. You will start to read your own feelings, or more accurately, you will start to recognize the emotions that you are creating and feeling. All emotion arises from the ego (attachment). Start by reflecting on your day and rewinding to the moments when you 'reacted' as opposed to consciously and calmly responded to anything or anyone. Then look within the reaction for the exact emotion. Name it. Then look behind and notice what you were attached to, and identifying with, in your own mind. Gradually you will cease becoming so easily attached and therefore emotionally reactive. It takes time and depends to a large extent on how interested you are. Unfortunately that usually depends on how unhappy/stressed you regularly feel!

I know in many situations/occasions I am wrong somewhere, but in order to protect myself there comes EGO. In the process of letting the ego take over I hurt others as well as myself, so how do I stop all this?

It helps to realize there is no right or wrong in terms of your perceptions and beliefs. No one is ever right or wrong – we all just have different points of view (viewing point!) at any given moment. And they will change too. We just get 'stuck' when we become attached to one particular point of view, i.e. a specific belief. Then we lose our sense of self 'in the belief' and anything that seems to contradict it is then perceived as a personal attack. We then label the other and their belief as 'wrong'. This is why there is so much conflict at all levels in the world today.

When we become attached, which means 'fixed upon' a specific point of view/belief then defensiveness will follow and eventually that defensiveness becomes an attack. The emotions that you create in your defensiveness or aggression are your signals that you are making a mistake and the mistake needs to be corrected. That starts with letting go of the 'I am right' belief, and being open to others points of view. Unfortunately most of us are so deeply programmed in the belief that there is 'right and wrong' that we jump up, even if it's only in our mind, and judge and condemn others for what we perceive as their wrongness. We lose our peace, we lose our capacity to care for the other, and we lose our happiness. But we can't see how we are doing that to our self so we blame and project our pain on to others. And thereby hangs the main reason why so many people make themselves so unhappy, so many times, every day. I'm sure you are familiar with that old refrain, "You can either be right, or you can be happy!".

Remember - the ego is neither negative nor positive, it's neither right nor wrong, good nor bad, it's just a 'mistake' that happens within our self when we identify with something that we are not, at that subtle mental level. But to correct the mistake I first have to be aware of the mistake. And that can be a challenge simply because it is sometimes so subtle.

Can I remove my ego totally?
Well you may notice there are moments when you have no ego. These are moments when you just accept everyone and everything as they are; moments when you are genuinely curious about something or someone; moments when you give of your self without wanting

anything in return. These are egoless moments. You are not attached to anything and you are not trying to project or defend any fabricated sense of identity. If you have had such moments, and I suspect most people have, then why not create more, more frequently and for longer? If you have lived such moments for a few minutes then why not a few hours, days, weeks etc. So yes why not total removal, eventually! But you can't manufacture such moments. This is what many try to do. They believe they are being spiritual and making some kind of spiritual effort by 'trying to be' more egoless. More humble. But you can't, that's just the ego again. All you can do is 'notice' your mistakes, notice what you are creating and putting in the way of you being you, of you being your authentic self. And then stop doing that. Then the natural egoless you, the natural humble, yet powerful you, will emerge from behind all the cloaks of attachment you have been wearing and hiding behind! Be interested, be aware, be curious, but above all be patient, be very patient, in this process of seeing exactly what's IN the way!

Over time, with spiritual practice, (meditation and contemplation) you will start to notice when and why and to what you become attached, and the false sense of self that you consequently create. The more you become aware the less power your miscreation will have over you, until one day, it will have no power, and then on another day, it will be no more.

How can a relationship work when only one person has EGO?

Not for very long I suspect. I presume you mean by 'relationship' two people being/living together. Simply because in a relationship it takes two to tango and if one changes their steps then the other usually either follows or leaves the dance floor! The one without the ego will be stronger internally and they may 'influence' the other to 'let go' so often that the one with the ego eventually changes and follows. The reality of relationships however is both will suffer from ego simply because there is usually some attachment and where there is attachment there will be ego.

Occasionally you may find a couple who are so cool and accepting of each other, so unreactive at whatever the other says or does, so trusting of each other and transparent with each other all the time, so unconditionally giving to each other, so free of all expectations of the other – but it has to be so rare! And even if they were in such an egoless state i.e. in a 'together but not attached' relationship, you would likely find that at a deeper level it was not real. And the moment you would find that out would be when one threatens to leave, actually leaves or dies i.e. leaves their body! If the other suffers in any way that means then there was/is attachment and therefore the mistake of investing one's self, one's identity 'in the other', which means ego! The world teaches us to believe that that kind of suffering is natural, but from a purely spiritual point of view, all suffering is unnatural. It's the sign of ego/attachment. It's not wrong or bad, it's real, it happens, but it's just another sign of ego at work.

Put it this way, when you are egoless you are in your natural spiritual state. You are being spirit itself, you are being your self as spirit, as soul, as self, whatever word you want to use for the 'I' that says 'I am'. In that state of consciousness you are no longer trying to be somebody, you have no need or inclination to get attached to anything. You know that everything and everyone comes and goes, like leaves grow, whither, fall and are blown away by the wind. The destiny of a leaf is exactly the same as the destiny of everything else in the world, including the bodies that we occupy. That's the most natural thing in the world. Now why would we cry about the most natural thing in the world? Because we don't know our self as spirit, we have forgotten how to be just 'beings'! And when we forget that we start to cling to and identify our self with 'the material', ever-changing, ever-decaying, ever-being blown away, things in the world. It starts with the dwelling we call 'my body'! Then it expands into other people's bodies i.e. our intimate relationships. That's why we suffer. That's why we 'emote' at each other! So it is seldom just one partner that has ego. Both usually do it, and then they blame each other for what they 'feel'!

Many, if not most, intimate relationships operate on a silent cost benefit analysis! The moments of irritation or frustration with the other are seen as both par for the course, and worth tolerating, to stave of the alternative which is loneliness or the stigma of society that comes with being seen to be alone! Until of course those irritations/frustrations become frequent and intense enough to sway the pendulum into a decision that the emotional costs now outweigh the relational benefits. Such are the ego's games, even in the context of an intimate relationship!

Is the subconscious part of the ego?

The subconscious is an aspect of consciousness. The subconscious is where you keep all the memories/recordings of all that you have created in the forms of thoughts, feelings, tendencies and habits. They are recorded but held outside of your moment-to-moment awareness within the repository of the subconscious. If they weren't then the noise and the chaos in your mind would literally drive you crazy. What you have created and held in your subconscious is what is sometimes called 'unfinished business'. It's all the forms of your miscreation. It's all the habits and thoughts and actions and intentions that you have created when you have NOT been in your true and natural state of consciousness, which is free of attachment and therefore peaceful and loving and joyful.

When you create any thought or action that is not aligned to the true you, has not arisen out of your true and pure state as a free being, then it is held in your consciousness, in your subconscious. It's a mistake or miscreation that is awaiting to be resolved or 'healed'. Unfortunately no one teaches us that or how to heal all the wounds (miscreations) within our consciousness. So we just create and accumulate more and more memories of misaligned thoughts, feelings and actions. Eventually the energy of all that accumulation may affect the physical energy that is our body and therefore the health of our body. It will also start to generate an almost constant stream of emotions thereby sabotaging our wellbeing.

That's why just about every being on the planet is not well in their being and that 'unwellness of being' will eventually take its toll on the health of the body! Any emotion is a sign you are, in that moment, not well. The physical health of your body might be OK, but you are not well in your being. (see the book The Immune System of the SOUL)

Love and joy, peace and contentment, are not emotions. They are natural states of being when there is no attachment, no ego and therefore no emotion. They are symptoms of wellness.

Is your subconscious also connected to our true nature?
When you are being your true self then the energy of your consciousness, which is you, is vibrating and radiating as what we call love or joy. And when you are in that state, then there is no subconscious. There is no need for a place to hold any records of your creation. Your creation, which are your thoughts and feelings are arising as love and joy and they find a way out into the world through your behavior. You are like a river and you are 'in flow'. The river leaves nothing behind it just carries everything forward in its flow. But if you dam a river then the river stops, gets stagnant and

becomes smelly. So the first moment you become attached to anything or anyone, that's the moment you place a dam in front of the river of the spiritual energy that is you. In that moment you are acting against your natural flow and that's the moment you will feel some form of suffering, which is the emotion of fear, the fear of losing what you have become attached to. Now you are in a state of fear, which is unnatural. It's not the true you. Stagnation and smelliness are inevitable... metaphorically speaking!

When you are in your natural state of consciousness, which is peaceful and loving, you have no inclination to hold onto anything. You don't need to. Why do people 'cling' today? Because they believe that what they cling to brings them some kind of peace and love and happiness. But seeking love and happiness in anything outside of your self only brings sadness, fear and anger!

We cling to the belief that peace/love/happiness come from the material things in life. Then we cling to the memorized stimulations that result from our material indulgences mistakenly believing them to be forms of peace/love/happiness. You remember the things and people, and your interactions with those things and people that you 'believed' brought you love and happiness. Now you are creating memories and you need a place to store those memories so you create a vault in your subconscious - a personal vault, full of memories and images and feelings, etc.

But those memories are based on two illusions. The first is that you are only a material entity and the second is that peace, happiness and love come from outside your self. That 'belief is not true'! So it will be the cause of further peacelessness in the form of many emotions and therefore much unhappiness. Which is then recorded in your subconscious awaiting the triggers that will re-activate them and make you suffer more. Until it's time to find a good therapist!

How do I stay stable and be a
detached observer all the time?

The practice of meditation will allow you to see and realize how you are attaching to, and identifying with, ideas and images, memories and concepts, and how that is causing your emotional instability. You will also start to see that you cannot own, possess, or hold onto anything or anyone. You don't need to. You can't anyway. Ultimately it's not possible to 'have' anything. These are realizations that come when you awaken to who you really are, which is, remember, no one! We are each a being living in and through a physical form. Keep reminding your self that 'I' am the 'I' that says 'I AM', and that anything after 'I AM' is not me. This body is not me, it's my dwelling, my vehicle, but it's not me. Gradually you will notice that by becoming attached to anyone or anything will always result in feelings of instability and insecurity. It's OK for a while, we can tolerate the instability for so long. Until...

Gradually, with practice, you will notice how you are able maintain that level of 'detached observation' in more and more situations.

How do you take the emotion out of the
equation when faced with challenges?

Well all emotion, as we have seen, arises from attachment (love is not an emotion!). Attachment arises from and sustains the 'belief' that I can possess/own something. That gives rise to desire, the thought, 'I want...'. Then, when we get what we want, we believe we have found happiness. But it's not, it's just a temporary stimulation that becomes an attachment that I then 'fear losing' or fear not getting again! 'I want' that job is the desire. There is a moment of stimulation when we get the job, which results in elation, which we mistakenly call happiness. Then we create the belief that the job is mine. Then comes the 'ego mistake' – the job is me! Then we spend much of our time and energy fearing losing the job or that what we do in our job will not be approved of.

So if you contemplate this 'process' it will eventually reveal to you the secret of a truly contented, joyful and happy being, which is to 'want nothing'! If you can be free of all desire then you will know peace and be fully available to give of your self, which is love, and that is what gives rise to true happiness. Peace is... love does... and happiness rewards. So when you are faced with any situation, or relationship, challenging or not, can you want nothing from the person or the situation? If you can truly want nothing and yet enter fully into the situation or relationship then you will remain emotionally free internally and that will allow you to be happy and give of your best. But if you want something for your self then fear and anger are always only moments away. Suffering and unhappiness is only a thought, a word, away. Which is, unfortunately, how most of 'learn' to live our entire life!

When a major disaster occurs surely there must be an emotional reaction and then the moment comes when you decide what to do?

True, but it seems many don't know how to separate the two. In other words the emotion becomes the shaper of the reactive behavior. It shapes the action, which is usually violent towards someone or something within the situation that has triggered (not caused) the emotion. Remember emotion is a violation of the true and natural state of the self. It just finds its way out into the world as a projection on to the other person/s or situation/s. The secret is to realize not only have I nothing to lose because nothing is ever 'mine', but also to realize there are no disasters, nothing bad ever happens. Stuff just happens. That doesn't mean the suffering of others is OK and they should be left to get on with it. On the contrary, suffering is a cry for help but we can only help if we ourselves are not suffering.

In others words, you can only care for others when you are not emotional our self. It's hard to wrap your head around that kind of reasoning and logic simply because we have been taught almost the opposite. Remember perception is both your reality and your choice. But it's only possible to 'perceive accurately' when you have awakened to who and what you really are! That's why one person's disaster can be another person's celebration. But to the enlightened soul it is neither! It's just another scene!

Should we not identify with virtues too?

You cannot identify with virtue/s, you cannot get attached to virtue. You can get attached to the 'idea' of virtue, or the idea of virtuous behavior, or the 'memory' of virtuous action, and many do. But that just becomes the basis of another, if somewhat subtle, face of the ego. You are not an idea or a memory. Virtue is love in action and love only acts when there is no attachment, no agenda, no desire for self. Being virtuous comes naturally when you are being your self, which is the same as being love! If you 'idealize' it you won't 'realize' it. You'll become attached to the ideal and then disappoint yourself whenever you realize you are not living up to the 'ideal'. Another of ego's games!

In a situation if I stick to being loveful someone may say I am attached to being loveful?

You cannot stick to it. As soon as you think I am being loveful you're not, in the truest sense. You are creating and attaching and identifying with an idea/image of 'being loveful', so the ego will form and you will know it's ego the moment you 'resent' any lack of recognition or appreciation for your lovefulness! Or when the other slightly rejects your apparent lovefulness you will become a little upset. That means it wasn't true love, it was just a manufactured ideal with which you identified your self. Ego again.

How can you still be determined or result oriented if there is no ego?

Yes, it's such a good question. Most people's determination is ego-driven. Most people who are driven by results are achievement-driven. That's why they tend to be pretty miserable on the way to the goal and then allow themselves a moment of euphoria only when they arrive/achieve. Then it's off again to the next achievement and more struggle and strain to get there. Plus, there is likely to be much fear of failure along the way! But if you challenge them they'll likely say. "But I like it this way, this is how life is lived, everyone does this, if you want to get on in life you have to set your goals and go for them". But to me that's just a programmed set of beliefs that guarantees life will not be a very happy one. Mind you, some believe the rewards from all the achievements, despite the stress along the way, will then be enough to buy a few weeks on the beach. That's when another crazy belief kicks in which says that, "It was worth the pain after all"!

But look closely and you'll notice how your sense of self is being shaped by an image in your mind of the actual result/achievement. Then you have to manifest that in front of others in order to get confirmation that you have achieved, in order to get their recognition, which you then use to bolster your self-esteem and self-worth. You're trying to be somebody! It's just a merry-go-round based on an image that is not the real you.

Determined people are often just stubborn people. They don't dare stop and question the validity of what they are doing because they know if they do then what they may discover could be a bit... scary! But there are those who have a quiet determination and a focused consistency in what they do. They are not doing it for show, for recognition or for some high that comes with achievement or results. They are doing it because it's the most accurate thing for them to do. That sense of accuracy comes from deep within their consciousness, from their heart, their self! They are aligned with their trueness, their authenticity, which arises from the heart of their being, not from the targets and trajectories they feel obliged to achieve for others in the world.

What's the difference between being free/peaceful and being complacent?

Being complacent means you don't care, you're lazy, you can't be bothered ensuring you create the most accurate response to people and life around you and the situations that you are facing. To care is an expression of love and that is only possible when you are at peace within your self. Our peace is disturbed by our attachments, by the thoughts 'I want' or 'why am I not getting' or 'I am about to lose something'. Then you just care about your self and don't bother so much about others. That is then interpreted by others as complacency, as uncaring. When you are free internally (no attachment) you will be at peace. Then you are not busy worrying about whether your desires will be fulfilled or not. Then you are naturally more available to care for others.

How do you detach? Isn't that a sign of weakness? Will there not be a loss?

Detachment does not mean you avoid or do not care. You simply change your relationship with the object/s of attachment. That takes place entirely within your consciousness. Instead of considering something to be 'mine' you realize, in truth, no one and no thing is ever 'mine'! At a more subtle level, when you practice meditation, the first step is 'detached observation'. This allows you to realize there is you and there is your mind and there is what is on your mind. You are not your mind and you are not what is on your mind. So you gradually break the habit of losing your sense of self in what's on your mind. What's on your mind is always changing, moving, coming and going. But you are still, the watcher, the witness, the observer. When you restore this inner 'position' you are detached. But you still engage and interact with the world. But now it is without emotion and with more... feeling! Now you are no longer vulnerable to others words and behaviors. Which means you 'stand in your power'. That is strength not weakness.

When you say I am nothing - is this not thinking low of our self?

When we look deeply into the ego and attachment and understand how we create all these 'selfs', so to speak, based on ideas and images in our mind, we always arrive back at the question 'well who am I'. If I am not the car, the job, the partner, the nationality etc., who on earth am I? When I answered that question at one point earlier today I didn't say you were 'nothing' I said you were 'no thing'! There is a difference.

Most people just believe they are their body, which is a thing, an object, so they objectify themselves. Then they start to identify with what they put on the body and around their body etc. More things. Then some will identify with an assimilated belief system or with their emotions, which are, within consciousness, just more 'things'. But you and I, we are not a thing. We are the creators of things as in creators of thoughts, feelings, ideas, beliefs, intentions, etc. – these are 'things' and we are the creator. But the creator is not a thing. Which is another way of saying you have no identity! No thing really means no one! It's a kind of paradox. When people hear that, they get very scared and start thinking that if they believe that then they will lose their identity. But they don't realize they are already losing their identity several hundred times every day. It's a wonderful irony, paradox, cosmic joke, huge mistake, call it what you will.

The ultimate freedom is to realize you are no one! But it seems it's not possible to fully realize this until we are ready. Until we have done our inner work. It's as if you cannot realize the reality of being no one until you have realized that trying to be someone is futile and an act against the truth of who you really are! You are certainly nobody as in 'not a body', but you are also 'a nobody', as in you are not a special somebody! When you realize that for your self, you are then free to be your self. But you can't think or theorize your way there. To become naked within your self is to be your self. All the false identities you create are like layers of clothing you are wearing on your body. They need to be 'cast off'. Then you become naked within. Not so easy after a lifetime of believing you are 'some body' and a 'somebody'!

Is ego only negative?

Ego is neither negative of positive. It is a creation of consciousness and there is no positive or negative within consciousness. It is simply a mistake in that we create an image in the mind and then lose our sense of self in the image and use the image to give our self our sense of identity. It's such a subtle movement within consciousness that we don't notice it most of the time. But, as we have seen, it is the cause of all suffering, all our stress, any and all sorrow, which is why it tends to be called negative.

If you slip into the negative versus positive mindset you then start thinking 'right and wrong', then it's 'good and bad'. But there is no good or bad 'in reality'. There are no bad people, just people who are not aware that they have created an ego and that it's from the ego, from that mistake, that their violence arises towards others. When you recognize and realize that, then it frees you from judgment and condemnation and that opens your consciousness, you, to compassion. But that's also not so easy as we have all been brilliantly conditioned to 'believe' in positive/negative, right/wrong, good/bad. Every day the world and people around us influence us back into that 'mindset'!

How can we create naturally and is this creation stepping away from reality or being naive e.g. if someone is mistreating you?

No one mistreats you! People just say and do what they say and do. Put it this way: *It's not what you say and do that makes me feel this way, it's what I do with what you say and do that makes me feel this way!* You only believe someone mistreats you because you 'believe' you should be treated in a certain way. You have an idea/image of how you 'should' be treated to which you are attached. It's desire again! You 'want' to be given certain treatment!

Then, when someone does not live up to the image that you are attached to, you create upsetness in some form of anger and then project it onto them. And if they are also not yet enlightened regarding such exchanges they will likely become upset at your treatment of them and then send it back to you, then you back to them, then them back to you. And how long does it go on for? In some cases, for a lifetime. Sometimes it's called marriage! ;-)

If we are no one with no intrinsic identity how do we live and operate in the world surrounded by people who seem so certain about who they are?

By speaking the international language of labels. Essentially all identities are labels that we give to our self, including gender, colour, age, nationality, profession, religion etc. These are labels and people speak from their label. So you learn to speak this language. But the difference is you don't identify with the label. I don't walk through passport control at the airport saying, as I show my passport, "Well it's not really me. I'm no one really"! No, you play the game and speak the language. But if your nationality label is 'British' and someone insults Britishness then it doesn't bother you one iota because deep within you there is no attachment to, or identification with, the label, the idea, the concept that we call British. From a spiritual point of view 'British' is just another idea! And I am not an idea!

So if we have no intrinsic identity, if we are in truth no one and no thing, what's the point of life, what's the purpose of living?

The purpose of life is so simple. It's almost too simple to realize, such is the complexity we have created and are used to in our life. The purpose of life is 'to live'. That naturally gives rise the next question which is 'how do I live'? How do I live in this physical world? Well everyone is already living their purpose, but the vast majority do not realise it. They either a) 'believe' there is no purpose, b) they don't know their purpose or c) they have to find their purpose. But you are already living it, every moment of your life. How do you know it? Take a moment. Sit quietly. And notice what you are doing at every moment, regardless of where you are or who you are with. You will see that you are 'thinking'. You are generating thought. Therefore you are a creator. Everything that you do starts in your mind with your thoughts. Therefore you are intrinsically creative.

So your purpose is to be creative. Not in an artistic sense. That's a very small and limited aspect of our idea of creativity. Some people sometimes say to others 'get a life', especially if they don't approve of the other! But I didn't come here to 'get a life'. I am here to 'create my life'. That's it. Then it's just a question of what is informing my creation, what is shaping my thoughts and decisions and choices. Is it the conditioning of others, is it the belief systems of others, or is it my self awareness, is it my own realizations, is it the deeper truths that I have realised that is informing how I create my life, my journey through life and what I manifest in life? Only you can know for yourself precisely the answer to that.

However, if you experience any sorrow, or stress, or suffering, then that is the signal that you are not creating in alignment with your 'trueness', you are miscreating! It's still creative but it's shaped by illusions, by a set of beliefs that are not true, usually by the influence and agendas of others. For most people it's other people and their influence that shapes how they create their life. Parents and teachers and politicians all have their agendas, which they try to achieve through us as we grow and live in the world. We inherit their attachments, their beliefs and perceptions, and because we saw them as authority figures we just blindly believed they were right! They were not right and they were not wrong, just asleep! Just unaware that they themselves were not creating their life free of attachment, free of ego, as free beings.

They had and mostly still have not realized there is no such thing as nationality, that we are not our race, that religious beliefs just become attachments that will hold us in conflict with each other as they generate fear and division where there is none! They were not and are still not aware that attachment to anything or anyone is guaranteed to create an unhappy life. They learned that love is attachment, that worrying is caring, that excitement is happiness. Then they handed those beliefs, those illusions, on to us. But you have to see and realise this for your self. Otherwise these words have no power.

As I said earlier, it's best not to 'believe' a word I say.

See for your self.

Where does God fit into finding our way beyond our ego and emotions?

Thought starts as a wave of energy that arises naturally from being. God is a being and you are a being. Waves of energy arise and emanate from you, as they do from the One, the Source, we call God. The difference is we give our waves a form and for that we create/emerge a 'mind' within our consciousness. We call them 'thought forms'. Whereas God does not need to give 'his waves' a form! So he does not need to create a mind. He just waves...so to speak! He just radiates light. By the way it's neither a He nor a She, as a spiritual being has no gender. He or She are used here for convenience and perhaps to not make it too impersonal.

God is forever radiating subtle waves of energy. Some call those waves spiritual light while others call them divine vibrations. Like the sun in the sky, God radiates this subtle spiritual energy in all directions at all times. It's just that in a spiritual dimension there is no direction and there is no time! Nevertheless, when we elevate our own vibrations we are able to catch those waves, those vibrations, and thereby create a direct personal connection with the ONE, with 'the Source', with the being that has been called by many names. We are able to bathe in the light of the spiritual sun. So why don't we?

The main reason is we create a mind within our being. Then, when we give the waves that emanate from our own being a form in our mind, we get busy with our 'thought forms'. We start thinking about our own thought forms and create more thought forms! Then we become attached to our thought forms as we try to preserve them. Then we lose our self 'in the forms' that we create. We are no longer 'available' and open to receive the waves of light from the source.

We become 'enclosed' within our thought forms within our mind. It's our thought forms that block those waves of radiant light from the penetrating our consciousness, so they cannot connect with our being, they cannot touch our heart. We become untouchable! And our heart withers away quietly within us. Sometimes not so quietly!

That's why if you want to connect to God, to the Source, you will need to keep waving, but stop giving form to your waves! That's the purpose of meditation, to stop creating thought forms from the waves of energy that are constantly emanating from the heart of your being. Then your light, which is you, is free to meet and receive the light and loving vibrations of the Source. Light connects with light. When your waves meet the waves of the Source, you feel something extremely beautiful. Often referred to as bliss.

This connection, this union, is also referred to as yoga. The more you connect and unite in such moments with the Source the less you need to think, and the less you create an ego, as you cease to attach to and identify with your own thought forms. The vibration of God as a being of spiritual energy is the same as our original vibration before we started attaching to images/ideas (thoughts) in our minds. The difference is God has not been influenced by the material world. That doesn't mean you never need to create thought forms. We obviously need to use our thoughts and therefore our minds to navigate the practical aspects of our day-to-day life in the world. But the quantity of 'thought forms' becomes less and the quality of 'thought forming' becomes greater.

The more you maintain that connection with the Source the more it reminds you and influences you to return back to your own original vibration as a source of the spiritual light we call peace and love. A kind of purification takes place as all the illusions are seen to be just that, illusions, and all the emotional wounds are gradually healed.

Establishing that connection requires the silencing of mental thought forming. Not in an inner struggle or resistance, but through a gentle meditative process whereby the self stops energising any thought forming activity, returns to the centre of the self and becomes still and silent. Then the heart starts to open, which is the equivalent of the flower silently and gracefully opening for and to the sun.

To do that you have to be out of your mind, literally! Hence the first practice of meditation is detached (from all mental creation) observation (of any arising memories).

Maintaining the connection means gently reminding oneself that the light of the Source is always available but that any attachment, any ego, will get in the way, will block the light. You naturally start to notice and check any inclination to attach. You avoid reinvigorating the ego. You notice and dissolve the inclination to become emotional. These are the signals the connection has been broken or is about to break.

Patience and practice 'in here', with the intention to be loving towards all of creation 'out there', gradually returns you to be what you have always been, which is your self!

Part 7

The Epilogue
and the Essence

Keeping it Simple

The Epilogue

There is a curious aspiration to be found in the declaration and constitution of a certain community in the world! It is expressed as: An 'unalienable right' to "Life, Liberty and the Pursuit of Happiness".

But on closer scrutiny, from a purely spiritual perspective, it doesn't really make much sense for the following reasons.

The Right to LIFE

Being alive is not a right that can be granted by any other. It is a responsibility to be fulfilled by oneself. From a spiritual point of view the right to be alive is irrelevant, as the self/soul/spirit is never not alive! How we live our life in the material world can only ever be a personal responsibility and the right 'not to be killed', which is really what this 'right' is pointing at, is at best illogical and at worst probably a bit daft!

The Right to LIBERTY

True freedom is not the ability to go anywhere, do or say anything. Liberation is an internal state of being when the self is not attached to anyone or any 'thing'. Only the self can deny the self it's own liberty. You can lock a body in a room but you can never lock the soul/self...anywhere! Being truly FREE is not a right, it can only ever be a personal responsibility!

The Right to Pursue HAPPINESS

If you 'pursue' happiness in almost any sense then you are guaranteed to make your self unhappy. To pursue happiness means to *search*, to *chase after*, to *look outside* of ones self for happiness. This is to look in the very place it can never be found. Ask most people, "Who is responsible for your happiness", and most will say, "Me, of course!" But two minutes later they will be upset with someone or something, which means they still carry the 'viral belief' that other people and situations are responsible for their happiness. Happiness is a decision not a dependency, it is an unpursuable self responsibility!

The Essence

Whenever you perceive someone or something as being 'in the way', it means you want something on the other side of the obstacle that they represent within your consciousness. Notice that whenever you desire something, whether it's an object, to be with someone, or for things to turn out the way you want, it's always because you are carrying a misbelief, an illusion, that when you get what you want only then can you be happy.

This belief is created the moment we lose our awareness of the truth about happiness, which reminds us that happiness comes from inside out, not outside in. We are each responsible for our own happiness. Many of us realise that particular truth 'in theory', but the habit of dependency is so strong, our beliefs and illusions about happiness are so powerful, we find it hard to live that truth.

But when you do, when you free your self from the idea that YOU have to get what YOU want, in order to be content and satisfied, then you will realize there never was anything IN the way except the belief itself. But the ego doesn't like that idea. It wants to remain attached, at least to that belief. It doesn't want to be freed from that belief, because if it is, it dies!

That's why, if you are ready to walk an authentic spiritual path you will need to be ready to embrace death in order to live! Death, in this context, means letting go of all that you are attached to, all that you desire, all that you basing your life upon. That's why some say life is just an opportunity to prepare well for death. They have realized themselves as spiritual entities and that death is not an end in itself but a passage that provides a bridge to the next chapter. It seems we all have to start dying well before we can start living ...well.

C'est la vie!

The Way

Most of us grow up believing
That there is always something
IN the Way
Whil many of us spend our entire life
Wrestling with perceived obstacles
It seems only a few will realize
That IN Reality
There IS nothing REAL
IN the Way
They are the ones who will
Tear down the curtains of illusion
Bringing clarity to their confusions
Dispelling their delusions
Ultimately helping others to see
There never was or is
Anything IN the Way
Only then can you be awakened
Only then can you BE Your Self
Only then can you be
Truly
ON YOUR Way!

If you have any questions regarding anything you have
read here please feel free to send them to me at
mike@relax7.com
I'll do my best to respond promptly.

Thanks and Links

Thanks to some of the most powerful and beautiful retreat centers where you can find the space 'to be' and the clarity 'to see', during many kinds of weekend retreats!

UK: www.globalretreatcentre.com

USA: (East Coast) www.peacevillageretreat.org

(West Coast) www.anubhutiretreatcenter.org

Australia: www.brahmakumaris.org/au/spiritual-retreats

Italy: www.casasangam.org

India: www.omshantiretreat.org; www.shantisarovar.org

Thanks to Lucinda and Andy for the kind of music that seeps into your heart and nourishes the soul.

www.blissfulmusic.com

Thanks to Marneta for showing us all how to reach the hearts of the children of the world.

www.relaxkids.com

Thanks to the BKs, where anyone can receive free tuition in meditation and begin anything from a simple meditation practice to a personal spiritual journey in centers in over 100 countries.

www.bkwsu.org

Gratitude to the Ammerdown Retreat Centre – an oasis of calm and tranquility in which to gather for an intimate retreat, as we do in August every year.

www.ammerdown.org

Deep appreciation for all the work of friends at Comic Relief as they carry both our cash and our compassion into a world of deprivation and violence that is the fate of so many children.

www.comicrelief.com

And finally, congratulations and gratitude to Piero for creating 'Santa Pasta', the new king of pastas – the healthiest, the tastiest, and made with the most elevated energies in the most organic way!

www.santapasta.it

About the Author

Mike George 'plays' a variety of roles including author, spiritual teacher, coach, management tutor, mentor and facilitator. He brings together the three key strands of 21st century - emotional/spiritual intelligence, leadership development and continuous 'unlearning'. In a unique blend of insight, wisdom and humor Mike entertains as he enlightens, speaks to your heart as he stay's out of your head and points to 'the way' as he waves you off on your journey!

Some of his previous books include:
The 7 Myths About LOVE... Actually!; The Immune System of the SOUL; Don't Get MAD Get Wise; The 7 AHA!s of Highly Enlightened Souls; In the Light of Meditation; Learn to Find Inner Peace; Learn to Relax.

Each year he leads awareness and enlightenment retreats across the world including Africa, Australia, Argentina, Brazil, Chile, Croatia, Germany, Italy, Mexico, Scandinavia, Spain and throughout the UK and USA

Mike can be contacted at **mike@relax7.com** and a schedule of his seminars and talks can usually be found at **www.relax7.com**

If you would like to receive Mike's regular e-article entitled
Clear Thinking you can subscribe at www.relax7.com - it's free.

For more of Mike's insights, workshops, retreats, seminars, talks, articles and meditations see:
www.relax7.com
www.mythsoflove.com
www.immunesystemofthesoul.com

CPSIA information can be obtained at www.ICGtesting.com
Printed in the USA
BVOW04s1316160514

353585BV00003B/3/P